CHOOSE YOUR PATH!

ATTACK ON TITAN

ADVENTURE

BY TOMOYUKI FUJINAMI
Illustrated by Ryosuke Fuji and Tetsu Yoshii
ATTACK ON TITAN CREATED BY HAJIME ISAYAMA

Prologue

This world belongs to the Titans.

Reduced to mere fodder for the giant creatures, humanity built three massive walls, and within them established a fragile peace and order.

But five years ago, in the year 845...

The first wall, Wall Maria, was destroyed when the Colossus Titan appeared.

A century of peace came to an end. Humanity lost a third of its territory and twenty percent of its population.

Now—the present day. The year 850.

The Colossus Titan has reappeared, near Trost District, the southernmost point of the second barrier, Wall Rose.

To prevent the tragedy of Wall Maria from happening again; to protect humanity's scant remaining land—Wall Rose must be defended to the death.

But our most experienced crack troops, the Survey Corps, are on an expedition far outside the wall. The defense will be mounted by the Garrison—and a Training Corps fresh out of boot camp will have to join them in battle...

This is an *Attack on Titan* adventure book.

You, the reader, will enter the world of *Attack on Titan* to fight and survive. You are the protagonist of this book. The choices you make will determine what happens in the story.

You are a member of the 104th Training Corps, a nameless soldier fighting in the Battle of Trost.

The battle against the overwhelmingly powerful Titans is not an easy one. A single wrong move could lead to your grisly death on the field.

However, with careful judgment and appropriate action, you can survive and even contribute to an eventual victory.

You may even save some of your friends who otherwise would be fated to die.

If you're ready, turn the page and start at section 1.

●1

A vast face appears from nowhere. Although it is human-shaped, it's also eerily skinless, its scarlet muscles standing exposed to the air. But you don't have even enough time to be distracted by its strangeness.

A stunning wave of steam hits you. Your vision goes white; you feel yourself being blown away.

Your mind feels as fogged as your vision. For a second, you don't know what's happening.

You are thrown into the air. You're more than 50 meters above the ground. Above you, the blue sky is oddly peaceful. Below, you can see the reddish-brown roofs of the town. From here, they look like toys. (Go to **2**.)

●2

You are 50 meters above the ground, but you won't be for long.

What do you do?

Flail in the air, looking for something to grab on to (Go to **3**)

Use some gas to propel yourself farther into the air (Go to **4**)

Use vertical maneuvering, set an anchor, and grapple along the wall (Go to **5**)

This is how the adventure proceeds. When you've decided what to do, turn the page and go to the number indicated.

•3

You find no handholds in the sky. There's a huge wall several meters away from you, but no matter how far you stretch out your arms you won't reach it. Helpless, you hit the ground and die.

(You have died. To retry, go **back to 2**)

•4

You let some gas out of the machine at your hip…but it doesn't change the speed of your fall. Someone more experienced might have been able to use the gas to effect a slight change in attitude, but it would not be enough to check the fall, or to fly. Someone more experienced… Someone more experienced in what?

Before you can remember, you strike the ground, shattering your body.

(You have died. To retry, go **back to 2**)

What is vertical maneuvering? What is an anchor?

You may not remember, but your body does.

Moving quickly in midair, you pull out the pistol-shaped control mechanism that had been in a holster at your side. You spin to face the wall, and pull the lever on the grip in your hand. Launchers on each side of you send out spear-tipped anchors. They bury themselves in the wall, trailing wires behind them. You stop falling and grapple against the wall. Pulling the trigger on the near side of your control device releases bursts of pressurized gas. A spool winds up the wires, and with its help, you plant your feet on the wall and begin to climb.

You remember: you can control your position in midair, in a way not only impossible but unthinkable for a normal person. You lean against the thin wires, with the device supporting your weight. This skill is what you have to show for three years of blood, sweat, and tears. (Go to **6**)

●6

If this…

Is your first time reading this, turn the page and go to 7

Is not your first time reading this, go to 96

You remember. You are part of the 104th Training Corps, stationed at the Wall Rose South District training camp.

There are camps to the east, west, south, and north, and you're at the one closest to the front line.

After three years of brutal training, you and your classmates are on the cusp of graduating and receiving your official —or at least, you were.

Why… Why now…?

You think back to just a few hours earlier, when Trost was a peaceful city.

****

How to Use this Book

This is an *Attack on Titan* adventure.

You take on the role of a member of the 104th Training Corps and participate in the Battle of Trost along with your classmates, including Eren and Mikasa.

You are the protagonist of this book.

This book explores an alternate history of *Attack on Titan*. What if you had been there? What if you had been a part of that battle?

The Battle Report Sheet

On page 12 of this book you will find a Battle Report Sheet.

When you find important clues in the story, or if you obtain an item, write it down here.

You may wish to use a pencil so you can erase what you've written.

Of course, you are not required to use this sheet. You can record things on a separate sheet of paper or in a notebook—or if you're confident in your powers of recall, you can fight without writing anything down.

You are a member of the 104th Training Corps. You're about the same age as your classmates like Eren and Mikasa—between 15 and 17 years old. You can pick your own name and gender, or you can leave them undetermined.

List of Comrades and "Affinity"

The Battle Report Sheet lists your brothers and sisters in arms—your classmates in the 104th Training Corps, as well as other soldiers on the battlefield with you. It doubles as a casualty register. If you see one of these people die in battle, or if you receive word of their death, put an X through their picture to indicate that they are dead.

You can also have a degree of **Affinity** with certain other characters. To start with, your **Affinity** with each other character is zero but may change due to actions you take during the story. You may wish to use tally marks to keep track of your **Affinity**.

Puzzles Hidden Throughout the Book

Throughout this book you will encounter puzzles such as codes and hidden words or numbers. Solving these puzzles may give you a chance to change your situation—or your destiny.

But this is the world of Attack on Titan, and these may not be letters and numbers that you would recognize. They are shown abstractly, demanding your powers of discernment and your ability to observe the battlefield. If you solve the puzzles, it means you've taken good stock of the situation on the ground, or have acted exceptionally.

This section will not explain exactly what form these puzzles will take. That is for you to discover on the field of battle.

Different Endings

This book depicts the Battle of Trost, seen in Volumes 1-4 of the *Attack on Titan* manga.

There are a number of possible endings.

Depending on your choices, you may receive a worse ending than that in the manga: humanity may be defeated, or characters who survived in the original version may die.

On the other hand, if you manage to survive the fight, you may get different endings based on your **Affinity** with various characters.

There is even the possibility that, if you solve the puzzles and truly distinguish yourself, the story may develop or conclude differently from the original; you may even be able to save your friends from a brutal death.

Everything depends on your choices.

Choose so that you are left with no regrets.

Are you ready? Then turn the page.

(Beginning on the next page, you will find the Battle Report Sheet, as well as Current Publicly Available Information that you may wish to know about this world. The story resumes with section 9 on page 16.)

ANNIE
LEONHART

BERTOLT
HOOVER

REINER
BRAUN

CONNIE
SPRINGER

MARCO
BOTT

FRANZ
KEFKA

HANNAH
DIAMANT

SQUAD 34
(THOMAS WAGNER /
MINA CAROLINA /
NAC TIUS /
MYLIUS ZERAMUSKI)

SURVEY CORPS   GARRISON

CAPTAIN
LEVI

RICO
BRZENSKA

IAN
DIETRICH

MITABI
JARNACH

MARK THE DEAD WITH AN X.

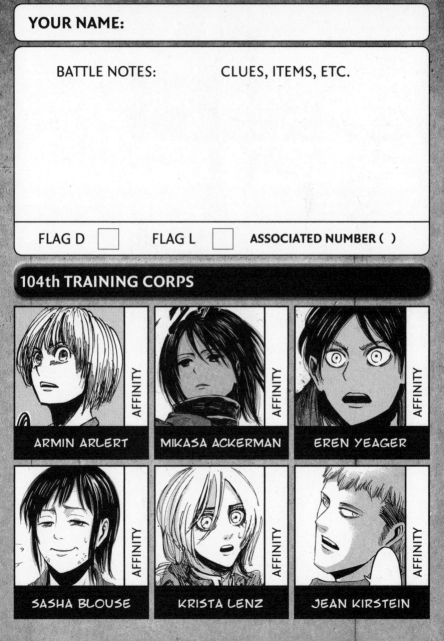

●8 – Current Publicly Available Information

Titans eat humans. That is, you.

Titans are of varying heights, from around two meters to 15-17 meters.

A 50-meter wall erected around humanity's remaining territory protected us for a hundred years, until, a 60-meter-tall "Colossus Titan" that appeared five years ago destroyed the wall.

It is unknown whether Titans are intelligent, but they appear to seek out and devour humans primarily by instinct. Where there are several humans present, a Titan will target the nearest one, or the largest group.

Their movements are sluggish and they walk slowly. (Larger Titans move considerably faster, due to their longer stride.)

Their faces show a single emotion, such as amusement, anger, or sadness, which never changes.

These Titans are referred to collectively as "Normal Types."

In contrast, some Titans do not conform to these basic tendencies; they are known as **"Abnormals."**

Though falling under the general category of Abnormals, these Titans possess a variety of characteristics. Some move quickly, others seem to show signs of intelligence, and still others do not seem to be drawn to humans.

The Colossus Titan may also be considered a unique variety of Titans do not attack non-human animals. Furthermore, they have survived for

NORMALLY STORED IN SIDE HOLSTER

CONTROL MECHANISM

WORN AT THIGH

SHEATH

WORN AT HIP

VERTICAL MANEUVERING EQUIPMENT

RAPID, THREE-DIMENSIONAL MOVEMENT IS THE GOAL. THE GEAR IS MADE AS LIGHT AS POSSIBLE.

a hundred years outside the walls without eating feeding on humans, suggesting they have no biological need for food.

Titan body temperatures are exceptionally high, and they possess powerful regenerative abilities. If they lose any limb, or even their head, they will regenerate it within a minute or two.

To kill a Titan, critical damage must be dealt to the nape of its neck.

The low accuracy of current human artillery makes it extremely difficult to target and fatally damage that specific spot.

For this reason, humanity has have a developed a battle tactic in which fighters maneuver behind the Titan and delivers a deep cut to the nape of the neck.

This is made possible by **Vertical Maneuvering Equipment.**

(When you have reviewed this information, go to 9. You may refer to this page at any time.)

●9 – On the City of Trost District

You are walking through the urban area known as Trost District.

You are a member of the 104th Training Corps. Your unit is based in Trost District, and for three years you have been training at a camp outside the city.

Trost is at the southernmost point of Wall Rose, the front line of humanity's defense. Your unit boasts that of the eight training corps attached to the various districts, yours is the most elite.

You remember the tragedy of five years ago—a century of peace shattered by the attack of the Colossus Titan, and the destruction of the first barrier, Wall Maria. Humanity was forced to flee deep into its territory, losing 20% of its population…

You were just a child then. That attack was the reason you joined the Training Corps. The training was painful and brutal, but all your classmates were good people.

There was the boy Eren, devoted to destroying every last Titan. The girl Mikasa, with her extraordinary physical abilities. Armin, a boy small in stature but great in intellect… There was the gentle, thoughtful Marco, while Reiner, reliable and brotherly, earned the trust of everyone in the unit. Annie was reticent and hard to get to know; but she excelled as a soldier. You'd like to enter the same regiment as her.

Silly Connie and ravenous Sasha were fun, too. Krista was always kind to everyone, and then there was the tall but timid Bertolt… You wonder what unit they all hope to join.

You found the bully Jean, and the two lovebirds, Hannah and Franz, to be a bit aloof. Yet now that you're all going your separate ways, you can't help but feel a little sad…

(When your classmates appear in this story, feel free to consult the Battle Record Sheet if you can't recall what they look like.)

You've survived three grueling years of training together; yesterday was the graduation ceremony. Tomorrow you'll apply to the unit you hope to join, and finally be a real soldier.

The units include the **Garrison**, which protects the people inside the wall; the **Military Police Brigade**, which guards the interior and the king; and the elite **Survey Corps**, which ventures outside the wall to do battle with the Titans…

You think about which unit you'll join, and about which units your classmates are likely to enter. (The path that leads to the **Military Police Brigade** is narrow; only the top ten trainees in a class are admitted into the unit.) But for the moment, you and the others are wandering around Trost District.

You have sundry duties to attend to, such as patrolling (that is, watching for enemy attacks) under the direction of the Garrison, and cleaning your weapons, but you don't presently have any training exercises, and are meandering around Trost in relative freedom. Maybe they want to give you a chance to catch your breath before you enter regular duty.

Taking advantage of the break, your classmates seem to have dispersed into town as well.

You look out at the town. The streets seem busier than they did when you first arrived here three years ago.

Now, where to go…

(Turn the page and choose where you want to go from section 10, the town map.)

19

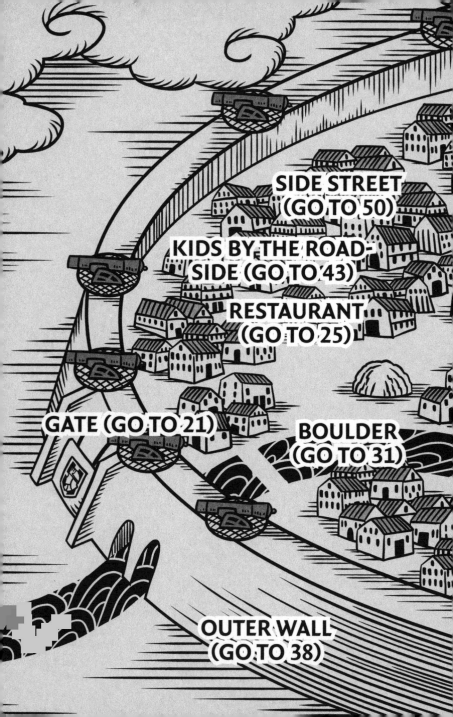

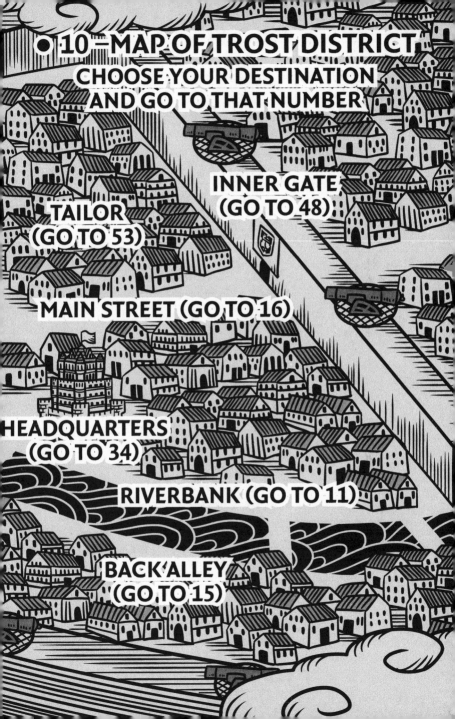

While walking along the riverbank, you spot your fellow trainee, Armin.

It looks like he's sitting and reading a book. He's smart, but you've heard rumors he reads forbidden books.

When you talk to him, Armin smiles. "It's not a forbidden book. Even I'm not crazy enough to walk around town carrying something like that. I'm not a kid anymore."

He shows you what he's reading. It's something technical. You recall that during training, any time he wasn't in class learning tactics or techniques, he was studying intently. You're impressed he managed it while still passing the training requirements. He's not just smart, he's a hard worker.

"What about you? Are you interested in books about…the outside world?"

You…

Are interested (Go to **23**)

Are not interested (Return to **the town map at 10** and choose a new destination)

●12

Hannah and Franz are talking excitedly together.

"You'd look beautiful no matter what you wore," says Franz.

Hannah responds, "I don't need a dress or a fancy wedding as long as I have you, Franz."

What a conversation. Apparently they're already making plans for their wedding.

Well, what can you expect from the the two notorious lovebirds?

(To talk to someone else, go back to **53**. To pick another destination, go back to the **town map at 10**.)

●13

You find yourself on a narrow side street well away from the broad main road.

Your fellow trainees Reiner, Bertolt, and Annie appear to be talking about something.

They were excellent trainees—all three of them made the top ten.

You hear Annie say "See you later, then," before she walks away.

Follow Annie (Go to **32**)

Approach Reiner and Bertolt (Go to **49**)

Go farther down the lonely side street (Go to **15**)

●14 – Dead End

You have died.

If you were lucky, your companions might have seen you die, and will report it so you can be registered among the fatalities.

If you're even luckier, they might be able to collect your body, or at least your personal effects, and return them to your remaining family.

Many who perish fighting the Titans don't even get that.

You may accept your death and rest from your struggle. If so, close the book now.

But…if you have the strength of heart to challenge the terrifying Titans once again, there is a way.

Return to the point immediately before your death and try again.

If you can't remember where you died, return to **1 or to the town map at 10**. You come to, not quite able to remember what happened, but feeling that you had a strange dream.

Alternatively, you can start again as another trainee (that is, another member of the 104th Training Corps, which has received word of your demise). In this case, reset your **Affinity** with each character to zero, but keep any flags and hidden numbers you've obtained. The things you achieved before your death benefit the new "you."

What happens to characters other than you who have died will depend on where you restart from.

Now, turn the page and return to your fight.

●15

You are in a narrow, dim back alley near the riverbank. You spot a newspaper lying on the ground as you walk. It's the Berg Newspaper, published in Stohess District, in the eastern part of Wall Sheena, far to the interior.

You pick it up to take a look, and spot the following headline: *"Survey Corps, Humanity's Hope, Launches 56th Expedition Beyond Wall."* And an article: *"104th Training Corps to become full soldiers at long last. We have high hopes for these stalwart young defenders."*

It's about you. You feel your chest puff out with pride.

Suddenly, you hear an angry voice from beside you.

"Newspapers, pah! Fulla lies!" It's a drunk man. "Like their 'Plan to Take Back Wall Maria' four years ago. Some plan! It was just a way to get rid of people they couldn't feed. Even kids know it—but will the papers write about it?"

He points at you and says: "Trainee, huh? Wonder what the papers'll say about *you* if things go south for the men in charge."

At that moment, another man approaches. He apologizes to you, and drags the drunk away.

"It's just the alcohol talking. Please, ignore him."

Then he turns to the first man, but you can still hear him:

"You better watch it. You go around talking like that, the MPs are going to take you in…"

(Return to the **town map at 10** and choose a new destination.)

●16

You're on the city's bustling main street. Vendors' stalls line both sides of the broad, stone-paved avenue, the place alive with locals walking around and doing their shopping. Carriages and carts rattle through from time to time.

You see your fellow trainees, Eren, Franz, and Hannah. They seem to be having a friendly chat.

"It's pretty lively here for a front-line city."

"Things are different from five years ago."

Talk to Eren (Go to **41**)

Talk to Franz and Hannah (Go to **26**)

Eavesdrop on passers-by (Go to **36**)

●17

"Eren? He definitely stood out, but not in a good way. Like, he was too serious. He had decent combat sense, though."

(Go to 33)

●18

You see Reiner not far away.

"Th-That would look great on her… She'd be beautiful…"

You completely agree, but Reiner does seem a bit creepy right now.

(To talk to someone else, go back to **53**. To choose a new destination, return to the **town map at 10**.)

●19

Annie's expression shifts ever so slightly. Then she shrugs and says, "Yeah, sure. I'm gonna apply to the Military Police Brigade and head for the interior. It'll be goodbye, boring frontier town." (Go to **46**)

●20

Your fellow trainee, Mikasa Ackerman, is there.

She stares silently at the dress, her black hair barely touching the old scarf she keeps wrapped around her neck.

She says nothing, and you can't tell what she's thinking. As usual.

You…

Say "I'll bet it'd look great on you too, Mikasa!" (Go to **51**)

Say "I'll bet you'd surprise the heck out of Eren if you wore that!" (Go to **35**)

Leave her alone and talk to someone else

(Go **back to 53**)

●21

The gate mounted in the city's outer wall is so large it can be seen from anywhere in town.

As suggested by the name "Wall Rose," a huge crest of the goddess Rose is emblazoned on it.

It is only when you approach the gate for yourself and gaze up at it that you realize just how big it is. Even cannons would barely scratch it, let alone a single human.

The gate is at once the border of human territory and a barrier against the Titans that roamed outside. There is a mechanism to raise and lower the gate, but it is hardly ever opened. These days, it is mainly used to accommodate the Survey Corps, who venture forth in efforts to learn about the world outside the wall.

In fact, just today…mere hours earlier, the Survey Corps set out from this gate.

(If you reflect on that moment, go to **22**. To choose a new destination, return to the **town map at 10**.)

●22

You think back to a few hours earlier.

The townspeople had turned out to see the Survey Corps off on another of their expeditions. You were among those who stood and watched them go.

The Survey Corps is composed of the most elite soldiers. Until five years ago, they were the only unit to have actual combat experience against the Titans. All of them were on horseback, followed by specially-built military supply wagons.

The number of soldiers and wagons seemed larger than usual this time. Perhaps they were planning an especially long expedition.

They looked so trustworthy. Their leader, Erwin, had gathered brave men and women of long service.

Captain Levi is particularly well-known. Rumor has it he's a one-man army… That's probably an exaggeration, but nonetheless, he seems to deserve his nickname of "humanity's strongest soldier."

When you saw him, you were taken aback by how small he was. He didn't look very friendly, though nothing else about him jumped out at you. But it's surprising how often the truly strong are like that.

The townspeople clamored. Many were cheering, but you also heard

more than a few shouts of "Why bother going outside the wall?" and "If you're such great soldiers, stay here so you can protect us when we need it!"

That's the scene you re-member.

(If you climb the outer

wall, go to **38**. To choose a new destination, return to the **town map at 10**.)

●**23**

When he realizes you're interested, Armin begins to talk.

"According to this book I read when I was a kid…"

It was a book about the outside world, and Armin says it mentioned fiery water, a continent of ice, snowbound deserts… He says a strange word, one you barely know: *sea*.

There's far more water in the "sea" than is in the canal.. Probably enough to cover the entire area inside the walls. In fact, apparently the majority of the outside world is "sea," and the land rose up out of it. But even though the land covers less than half the world's surface, there is still vastly more of it than is contained within the walls.

That tells you how big the "sea" must be—and it's salt water. So much salt the merchants could never squeeze it all out…

You can hardly imagine it. It's like a myth, or a flight of fancy.

You ask Armin if he really believes all that. He smiles sadly.

"In my mind…no," he says.

Maybe he really doesn't, or maybe he doesn't quite trust you. Having an interest in the world outside is considered taboo among the populace. It isn't expressly forbidden for military trainees, but neither is it smiled upon.

"But…it is true that that book gave me my interest in the outside world," says Armin.

He's choosing his words carefully, but he can't hide the light in his eyes.

"It might not be the dreamlike world from my book, but I'm certain the outside world is huge…and I want to see it for myself."

(Increase your **Affinity with Armin** by 1, and go to **24**.)

● **24**

Two other trainees approach. It's Eren and Mikasa.

"Hey," Eren says to you happily. "So you heard Armin's story too, huh? How about you join the Survey Corps with me, then? We'll exterminate the Titans and see what's outside!"

Armin smiles to see Eren this way.

If you remember correctly, Eren used to live in Shiganshina District, the one that was attacked by the Titans.

These three seem to share a special bond even for trainees: it isn't just that they're childhood friends, or what they've survived together. Maybe it's their drive to see the outside world.

Mikasa is looking at you with a stern expression.

You ask her which unit she wants to join, but she tells you it's none of your business.

(Return to **the town map at 10** and choose a new destination.)

•25

You find an eatery just off the main street, and it smells delicious.

You see your fellow trainee Sasha staring hungrily just outside the shop.

You think back to what you knew of her during training. She was always starving. She once stole a potato from the kitchen, an act the instructor made her pay dearly for.

She looks hungry as ever, right down to the thread of drool dangling from her mouth. Yuck...

"Hey," says an annoyed Connie as he goes by, "you're scaring the customers away. They're gonna run you off."

(If you **talk to Sasha**, go to **52**. If you **leave her be**, return to the map at **10** and choose a new destination.)

•26

Franz and Hannah are seriously in love with each other. Today they're walking along together, as usual.

In training, they'd been such an item that people started calling them "the lovebirds."

"What, you mean like husband and wife?" Franz would respond. "No way! It's way too soon for that!"

And Hannah: "Us, a nice couple? Eep!"

All right, they didn't say it. But their faces turned beet red. It was enough to embarrass you.

Today they're the same as always. You assume they'll apply to the same unit. Sometimes you found them grating in training, but the thought of not seeing their lovey-dovey faces again makes you a little sad.

(Go back to 16 and choose someone else to talk to, or return to the map at 10 and choose a new destination.)

●27

There's no sign of Annie Leonhart. She's probably not interested in a place like this.

(If you talk to someone else, go back to **53**. If you search for Annie elsewhere in town, return to **the town map at 10**.)

●28

As you prepare to leave, you notice some of your fellow trainees nearby.

It's Eren, Armin, and Mikasa.

You think you hear one of them say, "Just like we used to be."

They seem happy to be thinking of the past—but also somehow sad. You can't quite bring yourself to call out to them.

You remember the three of them are all survivors of the Titan attack that destroyed Shiganshina District five years ago.

They must have been so young. What hell did they witness…?

(Return to **the town map at 10** and choose a new destination.)

"The Military Police Brigade, obviously," Jean says, a little too loudly.

Come to think of it, all three of them were among the top ten scorers in your class. If they want, they could join the MPs, the king's elite guard unit.

"Why someone would want to join the Survey Corps is beyond me," Jean goes on with a smirk. "You guys know what I mean?"

Connie gives a click of his tongue. He seems a little miffed by Jean's attitude.

Indeed, Jean was not very well-liked in training, and his mouth was part of the reason. He seemed to particularly rub Eren the wrong way, and they often got into arguments and even fistfights.

"Hmm, yeah," Marco answers calmly. "I'm gonna go into the Military Police too. I've always really admired them."

The way he says it turns your stomach just a little. Marco is a thoughtful boy whose gentle personality, the polar opposite of Jean's, won him a lot of friends in the unit. Maybe he just said what he said to be polite— since only the top ten trainees can get into the MPs.

But you can't shake a sense of paradox: the better soldier someone is, the more likely they are to get tucked away in the Military Police Brigade, far from battle.

You think someone with Marco's character would make a great leader in combat…

(Return to **10** and choose again. There are other trainees you know just across the way—if you approach them, go to **16**. If you head away from the main street, go to **13**.)

•30

"…Hmph. Hand-to-hand combat isn't even part of our grade. As a soldier, you'll never need it." (Go to **33**)

•31

The city is home to a boulder the size of a small mountain. There appears to be excavation work going on, but it is a very large rock; even if the excavation succeeds, it will be hard to move. You can hear people talking in the street as they go by.

"They say the army's digging that rock out so they can use it to block up a hole if the wall is ever damaged."

"Yeah? And if they do dig it up, how are they gonna move it? The army…pfft. What a bunch of worthless freeloaders."

(Return to the **town map at 10** and choose a new destination.)

●32

Annie turns onto a deserted back street.

She's certainly a beautiful girl, with a good sense of style and gorgeous blonde hair, but her sharp features and hawkish nose give her an intimidating air. She has a keen look in her eyes, and doesn't seem eager to let anyone get close to her.

In training, she had been aloof and rarely showed emotion. She didn't seem to have any real friends. As you recall, she placed fourth in the class.

When you call out to her, Annie stops and looks back.

"Oh, it's you," she says disinterestedly. "What do you want?"

"Why do you want to join the MPs, Annie?" (Go to **42**)

"You have incredible fighting skills. Where did you learn them?" (Go to **30**)

"What do you think of Eren?" (Go to **17**)

●33

"Is that all you wanted to ask? If you're done, I'm gonna get out of here," Annie says.

(If you ask another question, go to **32**. If you end the conversation, return to **the town map at 10** and choose a new destination.)

You come to the city's military headquarters building. It's noticeably taller than most of the town's other structures. Its architecture is distinct, too, as it's a sturdy building made of stone. It reminds you of a fortress.

You count the windows and come up with seven floors, but floors one through four have high ceilings, making the headquarters even taller than you'd expect. The first floor is big enough for entire wagons to go in and out. It contains storage for supplies, gas tanks for vertical maneuvering equipment, and replacement parts, among other things.

It is both a supply base and the command center for the regiment that protects Trost District.

A swarm of soldiers mills around it.

"You one of the trainees?" an older soldier asks. The insignia on her chest shows the two-stemmed rose: she's a member of the Garrison.

You salute, and she returns the gesture. She has thick eyebrows and a knowing look behind a pair of spectacles.

Perhaps she knows you were just now taking in the building, because she looks up at it and says:

"The headquarters is built to last. It should hold even against a Titan attack. …Although if it ever has to, everything may already be lost."

(Return to **the town map at 10** and choose a new destination.)

●35

"…What?" Mikasa's eyes go unusually wide and she looks at you. "M-Maybe," she murmurs, a little embarrassed.

You're surprised to realize she has a soft side. (Go to **39**)

●36

You can hear the townspeople talking.

You hear some say: "It was awful five years ago, but things are peaceful now. And we have the soldiers to protect us."

But there are others:

"Sheesh. Just getting by is hard enough without those useless soldiers to feed."

(Go **back to 16** and pick again, or return to **the town map at 10** and choose a new destination.)

●37

Annie narrows her eyes and goes silent for a second, but soon says:

"Yeah. It's a habit from our combat exercises. I guess I don't need it now that our final grades are out."

That's right… On several occasions, they had you break up into squads and do a mock-combat exercise in which Trost was attacked by Titans.

She wasn't just wandering the city streets at random. This was probably how she'd learned the lay of the land, the buildings… That's what got her into the top scorers. (Go to **45**)

•38

A massive, 50-meter wall surrounds the city. Atop it you can see the fixed cannons and some soldiers on patrol. Here and there along the wall are elevators to carry people and materiel to the top.

Now—what do you do?

Your watch shift is beginning. Ascend the wall (Go to **54**)

There's still someplace you want to visit in town (Return to **the town map at 10** and choose a new destination.)

•39

You see Jean not far away.

"Her black hair would be perfect with that white dress," he's muttering. "Man, it was so long and beautiful…what a waste…"

Suddenly he glares at you.

"What're you looking at?"

(If you talk to someone else, go back to **53**. To choose a new destination, return to **the town map at 10**.)

Your fellow trainee, Krista Lenz, is there.

Krista is staring intently at the dress with her clear, blue eyes.

Is she…thinking of someone? You can't help but notice that with her golden hair and blue eyes, Krista is strikingly beautiful. That dress was made for a girl like her.

The freckled girl next to her says teasingly, "Is that longing I see?" The girl is another one of your classmates.

She had a sharp tongue, but she'd always gotten along with Krista. What was her name again?

Krista answers hesitantly, "I just… I was hoping he could have a happy wedding. I was thinking how I have to dedicate myself as a soldier to protecting people like this…"

"Hmph. Spoken like a true overachiever…" The freckled girl gives a defeated shrug. "Hey, Krista, don't you think that dress would look good on you? You'd probably look more like a princess than a bride, though…"

She laughs. The freckled girl's words are harsh, but there doesn't seem to be any malice behind them.

Krista… Krista makes an inscrutable expression. Maybe she's embarrassed?

(Go to **18**)

"Oh, hey," Eren says. "Have you decided which unit you're joining? I'm going into the Survey Corps, naturally—I'm gonna wipe out every last Titan!"

He's really worked up about this. Come to think of it, he was always like that in training, too.

"Oh, yeah," he adds, "don't forget you're on duty today. Come to the Outer Wall when it's time for your shift. Anyway, I'm gonna hit the town and enjoy our last chance to relax. Careful you don't spend all your time playing around!"

(Go **back to 16** and pick again, or return to **the town map at 10** and choose a new destination.)

●42

"...'Cause it'll get me to the interior." (Go to **33**)

●43

Some children are playing on the flagstones.

A few of them come over when they realize you're a trainee.

One is an outgoing boy; another boy seems quieter. A girl is with them. They must be about ten years old.

"Hey, you're a soldier, aren't you?" the energetic boy says, flushing.

"I saw the Survey Corps leaving through the gate this morning.

They're so cool! When I grow up, I'm gonna join 'em! I'll be just like Captain Levi!"

The girl comes closer, too. These kids seem to be obsessed with soldiers.

You can't help feeling a bit pleased.

"You and your friends…" the girl says. "You'll beat the Titans for us, right?"

The quiet boy, probably a friend of the other two, speaks to you hesitantly:

"The Titans are scary…but I want to see what's outside the wall," he says. "There's supposed to be way more space outside the walls than inside them. If we had vehicles that could fly through the air like a bird, maybe we could go outside without running into the Titans…"

A flying vehicle? Kids get the strangest ideas in their heads. Some-

thing like that sure would make fighting and studying the Titans easier, though.

(Best keep moving. Go to **28**.)

•44

You realize that while Annie seems disinterested at first glance, in reality she's carefully observing everything around her.

She's not just taking in the sights. She's studying every building's location and height, trying to commit them to memory.

What do you say to her?

"Making sure you remember this place?" (go to **19**)

"Thinking about what to do if there's a battle in Trost?" (go to **37**)

•45

"...I put a lot of effort into the combat exercises because they were worth a lot in our grades," she says with a shrug. Maybe she means Titans would never really attack Trost...or that it doesn't matter to her. (Go to **46**)

•46

Even in training, Annie Leonhart had seemed aloof. It was almost as if she didn't trust the rest of you. Not like your other classmates—especially Marco Bott.

"I'm just making sure I take care of myself," she continues, as if reading your mind. "When you're in combat, there are no guarantees your comrades will do what you'd hope they would. They may not be bad people, but they're as likely to freeze in fear as they are to keep a cool head."

She stares at you for a moment, then says:

"It looks like you're a pretty sharp observer yourself… Just be careful you don't rush to get yourself killed, trying to be a hero."

(If you take Annie's words to heart…go to **47**. Otherwise, return to **the town map at 10** and choose a new destination.)

•47

When you encounter the phrase "he/she seems somehow uneasy," you may add **4** to the number of that section and go to that passage instead, if you wish.

Remember or make a note of this. (Return to **the town map at 10** and choose a new destination.)

North of the wall that surrounds the city, the wall that borders the rest of humanity's territory is known as the inner wall, or rear wall.

Hence, the gate in the wall is known as the "inner gate."

The gate is emblazoned with a crest showing the profile of the goddess Rose, the symbol of the wall that bears her name.

Beyond the inner gate is another urban area, and beyond that, fields and forests and villages. Follow the road north, and you will come to Ehrmich District at Wall Sheena.

The gate to the interior is a mirror of the gate to the outside: while the latter stays closed and is hardly ever opened, the former stays open and is rarely closed. Many come and go through it, including travelers and merchants, as well as those who commute to the farms near the city. When you and your regiment came to your training camp, it was this gate that you came through.

Compared to the outer gate, which is patrolled by the Garrison, the inner gate is all but unguarded.

This gate and wall would also serve as a last line of defense were Trost's outer wall ever to be compromised. The inner wall, like the outer one, bears fixed artillery emplacements. Though you hope humanity will never need to use them…

(If you head toward the outer gate, go to **21**. To choose a new destination, go **back to the town map at 10**.)

Reiner is well-built and gives the impression of a reliable older brother. Bertolt, in contrast, is taller, but comes across as timid. Although opposites, they're also friends, and you often see them together.

At the moment, they're talking about something as they take in the town. Maybe it's for combat exercises. Not that they need to worry about those, now that you've all graduated…

When you call out, Bertolt seems oddly flustered.

"O-Oh," he starts, "W-We're going to leave this place soon, and it's just a little…"

Reiner breaks in with his usual coolness: "We were thinking about what would happen if Titans attacked."

"R-Reiner, what are you talking about?" For some reason, Bertolt seems more and more upset, but Reiner, looking serious, goes on:

"Is it that strange? We're soldiers. We have to be ready for anything."

He's right. Sometimes Reiner can seem a bit too serious, but he was one of the top graduates.

(If you go to look for Annie, go to **32**. To choose a new destination, go back to **the town map at 10**.)

●50

You're on a major road through town. You see a wide, flagstone-paved side street, crowded with carts and wagons. Along the street are places to unload cargo. Buildings, shops, and warehouses abound.

You see your fellow trainees Jean and Marco, along with the shaven-pated Connie.

The three of them appear to be discussing what unit they want to join.

(If you talk to them, go to **29**. To choose a new destination, go back to **the town map at 10**.)

●51

"…I doubt it. Besides, it would be hard to move in."

Mikasa responds without a change of expression, in her usual detached tone. Then she touches the old scarf she's wearing and murmurs, "It wouldn't suit me at all." (Go to **39**)

●52

A man who looks like the owner comes out of the restaurant.

"You're trainees, aren't you? Our future protectors are welcome to a meal on me."

He shows you to a table and brings out a steaming dish.

"Y-Y-You're the real hero!" Sasha says with tears in her eyes, and falls upon the plate.

"No need to be shy, kids," he says—and you and Connie end up with bowls, too.

It's sure better than the stuff they served at the training camp. It's a potato stew—nothing fancy, but it brings home how prosperous this town is, and how genuine your host.

"Umm," Sasha says, "there wouldn't happen to be any meat around, would there?"

"It's free food! Beggars can't be choosers!" Connie says, giving her a bop on the head.

But the shop owner just laughs, not bothered at all.

"Since our territory shrank five years ago, there have been strict limits on the number of livestock. Even in this city, meat's just for the richest merchants—or the highest-ranking soldiers."

(You, Sasha, and Connie thank the man profusely. Return to **the town map at 10** and choose a new destination.)

●53

A tailor's shop faces the street. Here, women's dresses and gentlemen's suits are made to order.

Places like this must be where the wealthy have their clothes made. The fact that it's here is proof of how well Trost is doing. Not that it has much to do with you. During training camp, you wore your military uniform all the time; the only civilian outfit you had was some old clothes you used as pajamas. Even once you're assigned to your new unit, you probably won't need to have new clothes made, even for your days off.

Some of your fellow trainees are outside the shop, peering in.

You take a look, too. You see a dresser and a mannequin torso, along with clothes and fabric on display.

You also see a young woman in a pure white dress.

An older woman, probably one of the employees, is smiling and pinning the dress.

The young woman must be having her bridal gown fitted.

She doesn't look poor, but neither does she seem especially rich—having this dress made is probably a once-in-a-lifetime event for her.

Which of your friends do you notice?

Annie (go to **27**)

Hannah (go to **12**)

Mikasa (go to **20**)

Krista (go to **40**)

You are on top of the outer wall of Trost District, 50 meters above the ground.

This is the southernmost point of Wall Rose, directly above the gate.

The top of the wall is about ten meters wide—that is to say, such is the wall's thickness.

A rail runs along the wall, with the "walltop fixed cannons" mounted on it. They can be moved along the rail, and are fixed into place to be fired. Your unit's duties include patrol of the wall top and maintenance of these guns.

You, along with Eren and Connie, are on duty now.

"I wanna join the Survey Corps," Connie says as he cleans a cannon. "At least then I wouldn't be in the same unit as Jean!"

So he says, anyway, but you suspect Eren's influence. More than a few people have decided they want to join the Survey Corps because they were moved by Eren's passion.

Some of Eren's squadmates—Thomas, Nac, and Mina—are working on nearby guns, and come to join the conversation.

"Say, everyone…" Sasha says. "I borrowed a little meat from the senior officers' private stock. Let's all share it together." She pulls a hunk of ham out of her pack.

Your comrades offer various astonished remarks.

"That's dumb even for you!"

"You wanna get tossed in the stocks?!"

You're just about to get your unit assignments. What is she thinking?

Since the Titan attack five years ago, meat has become a precious commodity on account of humanity's diminished territory. She's committed a serious violation.

"It's fine," Sasha says easily, putting the meat away with a smile. "Once we take our land back, we can raise more cows and sheep, too…"

All the others look startled.

"I get it," says Thomas. "A little pre-celebration for the retaking of Wall Maria."

Humanity will retake Wall Maria, which it lost to the Titans, and it is you newly-minted soldiers who will do it.

The thought spreads among those of you gathered on the wall. Of what Sasha has done, but also why. Then again, maybe she was just hungry.

Everyone pipes up once more.

"Well, then, I'll have some of that meat, too!"

"Save some for me!"

Defeating the Titans, taking back Wall Maria… It sounds like a dream, but with these people by your side, you think maybe you can do it.

No—you're *sure* you can. (Go to 55)

From the heights of the outer wall, you can see the world outside Wall Rose.

Near the wall is an abandoned city. There were people there until five years ago.

No one lives there now, but it remains surprisingly well-kept; from a distance it could be mistaken for a normal town. Titans attack humans, not empty buildings.

In the far distance, a great mountain range rises up to meet the sky. You know Wall Maria, ruined five years ago, must be out there as well, but even a wall 50 meters high fades into the horizon from here. Such is the scope of what humanity has lost.

The sky vaults above your head and reaches out farther than you can see, clear and blue.

You look out at the town that spreads out beneath that peaceful sky. It could almost be filled with people living normal lives.

Just sky, sky, sky, and the mountains far away.

Then, suddenly…

With no warning, a giant face appears.

It's a head taller than even the 50-meter wall—the Colossus Titan.
(Return to 1.)

You've made it back to the top of the wall…but now you realize that the spot just beneath your feet has a huge gouge in it.

It must be from where the Colossus Titan's arm struck the wall. You see the twisted remains of the cannon rail; of the guns themselves, there is no sign.

Beyond the wall you can see the Colossus Titan, its exposed muscles obscured by clouds of scalding steam.

You see Eren, facing this impossibly large opponent with his swords drawn.

You…

Leap into the fray to help Eren
(Go to **129**)

Can only watch
(Go to **64**)

Seize the moment to help your injured friends (Go to **97**)

•57

You are assigned to the outer wall—the front line.

Your orders are to join up with the front line troops, aid them in executing any battle plans and get the lay of the land, then report back as needed.

However, you are told, this is also the most dangerous area of operations. Only those who wish to go will be sent there.

(If you're having second thoughts, go back to **the map at 60** and choose a new destination. If you find the courage to volunteer, go to **163**.)

•58

As you watch dumbly, you see Eren rise, against every expectation. He flies crazily with the vertical maneuvering equipment, snatching Armin from the Titan's mouth. But it costs him his balance, and he winds up in the creature's jaws instead.

You marvel that he has managed any of this with only one leg.

"You think I'll die here? Like this?"

He sounds so strong. ...But in the same instant, the Titan closes its mouth as if it has not heard him.

Armin reaches out his hand. Just beyond his grasp, Eren's right arm, bitten off, falls uselessly to the ground. (Go to **257**)

The steam finally clears.

Atop the ruined wall stands Eren.

Your friends rejoin you. On the other side of the wall, there's no sign of the Colossus Titan— only sky.

Did Eren kill it? For a second you think he may have, but Eren himself is staring vacantly into space.

"It's just like five years ago. It suddenly appears…and suddenly vanishes."

There is much about Titans that is not well understood. Could such a Titan exist?

At the moment, more pressing than the riddle of the Colossus Titan is the fact that the gate has been destroyed.

A terrible hole gapes in it. The emergency materials will never be enough to cover it.

What's more, all the fixed guns just above the gate have been smashed.

It won't be long before Titans overrun the city.

"Trainees!"

Veteran soldiers from the Garrison rush up, landing nearby with their vertical maneuvering equipment.

"A plan has been put into effect with the appearance of the Colossus Titan. We're the vanguard squad. Leave the wall to us. You're to get back to headquarters, make your report, then follow whatever orders you're given."

You and your friends salute, then head down into the city.

Wheeled canons have been pulled out onto the main street.

They've been lined up in front of the shattered gate to meet the inevitable Titan incursion.

You head for the headquarters building deep in the city.

The clanging of a bell reverberates throughout town, announcing the state of emergency.

"Please evacuate as we have drilled! Leave all personal belongings behind!" The announcement can be heard far and wide.

"It'll be all right," somebody mutters. "It's not like five years ago. We've planned for the Colossus Titan, for a Titan attack. We've got a strategy. We've trained. This won't be like Shiganshina District five years ago…"

But you can hear the tremble in their voice. (Go to **61**)

WHERE ARE YOU ASSIGNED? CHOOSE, THEN GO TO THAT NUMBER.

MIDDLE GUARD
(GO TO 62)
SQUAD 34
EREN
ARMIN

MIDDLE GROUP

REAR GROUP
GUARD THE REAR, EVACUATE CITIZENS
(GO TO 119)
MIKASA

MIDDLE GUARD
(GO TO 74)
JEAN
KRISTA
SASHA

You are at the Trost District headquarters.

Headquarters personnel are standing at attention, receiving their orders, making their preparations, and then leaving.

You and the other trainees are there too.

"Our strategy has been decided. We help the citizens evacuate safely out the back, meeting the Titan invasion from the front. Unfortunately, our most experienced troops, the Survey Corps, are currently on assignment outside the wall. The Garrison will have to execute the plan by themselves."

A superior officer is giving orders.

"Trainees, you are to participate in the action with the Garrison. All of you succeeded in your graduation exercises. I expect you to succeed in this mission as well."

You and your comrades salute just as you learned in training.

It's the salute of every soldier: you make a fist with your right hand and place it over your chest. It shows that your heart is dedicated to the cause.

Throughout the headquarters, crowds of soldiers are hurriedly preparing to move out.

All around, you can hear the fear as your classmates talk. Jean is especially upset. His face is pale.

"Damn," he mutters. "Why did it have to be today? I would've been in the interior tomorrow!"

"I will protect you," Franz says to Hannah. But his voice is shaking. (Go to **60**)

•62

You are assigned to Squad 34 with Eren and Armin, just as you were in the combat exercises.

Eren calls out to the members of the squad with an incongruous smile.

"This is a good opportunity, don't you think? I mean, if we prove ourselves in this first battle before applying for the Survey Corps, watch how fast we get promoted up the ladder!"

Not to be outdone, your other comrades put in their two cents:

"You better believe we'll keep up our end of the fight! There's a lot of future Survey Corps members this time around!"

"All right, let's just see who takes out the most Titans!"

Thomas, Mina, Nac, Mylius…everyone in the squad is itching to get to work. Only Armin seems too nervous to say anything…

With Eren and the others by your side, you're sure you can win. (Go to **115**)

•63

Your body is dark with cannon smoke and ash, and your ears ring from the explosions as the guns fire on.

But the encroaching horde of Titans doesn't stop...

Do you continue the barrage (go to **218**) or return to the rear to make a report (go to **222**)?

•64

You can't make yourself move. You've heard about the Colossus Titan, but now, here, it hardly seems real. It is many times bigger than the Titan dummies you often faced off with in training. Steam that burns like fire rolls off its body. Facing it, Eren looks like a fly attacking a human. You can only marvel at his courage... (Go to **152**)

•65

You take off running. You use your vertical maneuvering equipment to get onto a nearby building, from which you set your anchors in the outer wall and start up. The faint voices of dying soldiers drift up to you from below, but you block them out and make for the top alone. (Go to **280**)

•66

"All right. It's a lot to handle...but I'll try."

Marco gives everyone detailed instructions. Even the perennially ill-tempered Jean obediently follows his orders. It must be the warmth of

Marco's personality.

"Just stay calm and do what we did in training. We'll take that Titan over there first." He pauses. "I'll be the bait." (Go to **219**)

•67

The retreat bell sounds at long last.

"A lot of people didn't make it… But I'm so grateful we were able to help our friends," Krista murmurs, pain tingeing the smile on her face.

You pass through the inner wall, into safety. (Increase your **Affinity with Krista** by **1** and go to **91**)

•68

The merchant shows no fear of Mikasa, but shouts boldly, "Just try it!! I'm the boss of this town's merchant association! And I go way back with your employer! A single word from me can decide what happens to a grunt like you!"

"And how would a dead man say a word?"

Mikasa has a strange look on her face. She isn't trying to intimidate the merchant; she's genuinely curious.

"B-Boss," says one of the man's subordinates, pale.

The merchant finally caves, and orders his lackeys to pull the cart back and open the road.

The assembled crowd gives a cheer. (Go to **83**)

As you advance into the city, you see destroyed buildings and the scattered corpses of soldiers.

You see the Titans, too. There seems to have been an epic battle here on the front lines.

(You receive a report of your comrades who died in the line of duty. Mark Franz Kefka and Hannah Diamant dead.)

You see human shapes on the roofs of buildings all around the city center. They are your classmates from the Training Corps.

This is strange… The retreat bell should have been audible from here, but no one has moved from the rooftops.

Mikasa has noticed it, too. She lands on one of the rooftops.

You see the faces of the Training Corps. Jean and Connie. All of them look utterly defeated.

You spot Armin. You're sure he was part of Squad 34 with Eren and the others…

He's sitting on the roof, his face bloodless.

"You're not hurt? Thank goodness you're all right," Mikasa says, walking up to him. "Where's the rest of Squad 34?" (Go to **70**)

Armin can barely squeeze out an answer:

"Those five carried out their mission…and died bravely in battle…"

You think there must be a better way to tell an old friend about the death of someone to whom she was so close, but you can't imagine what it might be.

"Eren… He went into that Titan's mouth, instead of me… To protect me…" Armin says, half speaking, half crying.

(**Mark Eren Yeager and Squad 34 dead**.)

You…

Criticize Armin (Go to 76)

Comfort Mikasa (Go to 177)

Suggest a rescue attempt (Go to 234)

●71

When you come to, you are lying on your side. Your body is shredded; half of it you can't even feel. Strangely, there is no pain.

Krista is holding you and heaving with sobs.

It looks like you managed to protect her.

She's beautiful, angelic, and she's weeping for you.

This sure is a better way to go than tumbling into some Titan's gullet… (Go to 14)

You see soldiers firing the walltop guns.

They're aiming for the Titans streaming through the hole in the gate, but the distance is impairing their accuracy. Few of their shots strike home.

The soldiers' mood is as dark as the smoke that billows from the cannons.

"Shit! We're not even gonna hold them up at this rate!"

"The vanguard squad was our best hope…and they're gone…"

"We might've been able to resist if the Survey Corps was here. I can't believe an attack came the day they left!"

"I wish we still had the guns on the outer wall. We could've at least shot down at the Titans coming in."

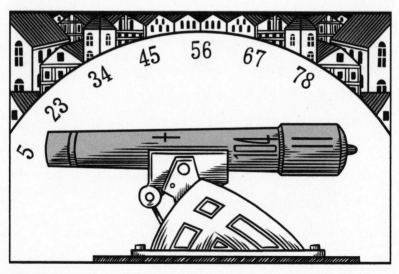

"If you got time to whine, you got time to shoot! Load cannons!"

They can't stop the Titan invasion.

On the ground below, the wheeled cannons are overrun; you hear the cries of men and women dying.

You…

Help with the cannons (Go to **109**)

Try to get word to the Survey Corps (Go to **146**)

Descend to ground level (Go to **78**)

•73

You spot a trainee coming back from the front. It's Armin.

"Armin…are you alone? What happened to the rest of your squad?"

Armin, pale as the grave, falls to his knees. You realize Squad 34 has been wiped out.

(Mark Eren Yeager and Squad 34 dead.)

Jean, his expression pained, mutters, "That kid had a death wish… I told him this would happen!"

Reports of soldiers killed in action are coming in from all over. There's more than you could have imagined. Trainees whose faces you knew are dying one after another. You hear Franz and Hannah's names among them.

(Mark Franz Kefka and Hannah Diamant dead.)

Jean, grinding his teeth, says only: "Damn!" (Go to **245**)

•74

You are assigned to the middle guard, as you were in combat exercises.

You take in the members of your squad and the squads nearby.

Jean, Krista, Sasha, Marco, Connie, and others, all familiar faces. You don't see Mikasa, Annie, Reiner, or the other top trainees. They must have been assigned to more important positions. You see Eren's Squad 34 head for the front, full of fight.

You and your comrades here may not be the top of your class, but you'll have to get the job done. (Go to 172)

•75

You can barely bring yourself to do it—but you leave him behind. You have no choice.

Krista moves to help him, but you hold her back yourself.

Later, you link up with Jean and Connie, and a few others. It looks like they managed to survive, too. (Go to 165).

•76

You ask Armin why he ran away, alone.

He has nothing to say, but only hangs his head in shame and quavers.

Mikasa shoves you out of the way. "I'm glad you're alive," she says to Armin. (Go to 177)

●77

You and your comrades do an exemplary job of bringing down the Titans.

When you stop to see whom you've saved, you find they're also trainees. (Go to 128)

●78

If you refuse to hide, alone, and go to the ground to help your friends, go to 123.

If you think you can best help where you are, go back to 72 and choose again.

●79

You decide to let Krista give the orders…what do you do?

Work to protect Krista (Go to 99)

Avoid attacking, but try to provide relief (Go to 148)

Hope she and her goody two-shoes act will get in trouble (Go to 168)

On your way to the rear, you run into Armin, standing in a torpor on a rooftop.

"What's wrong? Are you alone?" one of your comrades asks. Armin tells you that the rest of his squad has been wiped out.

The bile rises in your throat. That was Eren's squad.

"I'm glad you survived, even if you're the only one," Krista says, trying to comfort him. But the twisting in his face suggests her words hurt him more than ever.

He turns to your squad.

"Please," he says, "take my report to headquarters. I'm going back to the field." Without waiting for an answer, he launches off with his vertical maneuvering equipment.

Your squad falls back toward the rear, bringing the broken Hannah with them.

The retreat bell sounds at long last.

You and the other soldiers in the rear pass through the inner wall, withdrawing into safety...

(**Mark Eren Yeager and Squad 34 dead** and go to **91**.)

Mikasa seems to be worried about Eren, elsewhere on the battlefield.

"If I don't protect him...he'll get in trouble," she murmurs.

True, Eren is all too ready to rush in headlong...

What do you say to Mikasa?

"If you're a real soldier, then obey orders and do your duty." (Go to **169**)

"It's Eren, he'll be fine!" (Go to **103**)

"I'll create a diversion; you go find Eren!" (Go to **211**)

And so you act on the plan.

Thankfully, it achieved its goals. But the sacrifice to do so was immense. Almost eighty percent of your comrades died.

You and many of the others were decoys. You had nothing to do but flee. You were literally fodder. You saw friend after friend snatched from beside you and eaten by Titans. Titans in the 3-to-4-meter class don't swallow humans whole. They tear the living bodies apart and gnaw on bleeding flesh.

You could do nothing. Nothing but run.

That you are alive now is only a bit of luck. Good luck or bad, you can't tell.

(On your Battle Record Sheet, mark any four remaining members of the 104th Training Corps dead. As Krista was not on the field, you cannot choose her. Squad 34 counts as one person.

From this point on, those dead characters do not appear. Where they are mentioned in the narration, consider it your fond imagination of what they would have said or done, had they been alive. In addition, you may not pick choices that involve conversing or interacting with these dead characters. If this ever leaves you with no choices, go to 14 and start again.

When you have completed these instructions, go to 284.)

The evacuation resumes, and Mikasa returns to her position.

You hurry to direct the evacuees, and help those who have been slow to flee. You're extremely concerned about another Titan attack, but thankfully, nothing serious follows. Thanks to Mikasa's actions, and the lives of many soldiers, the Titan invasion has been stopped.

Finally, the evacuation is complete.

"Close the gate!" With that order, the gate on the inner wall, and the route to the interior, is sealed.

You finally relax. A bell rings out. The soldiers in the city have been given the order to retreat.

"Give it some gas! All hands over the wall, retreat!"

The commander at your position gives the order, and you use your vertical maneuvering equipment to climb onto a rooftop. You find Mikasa there.

"The evacuation...is complete." She looks out at the city, her back to you. Then she says to the Garrison soldiers, "I'm going to go support the front line's withdrawal."

You...

Follow Mikasa (Go to **149**)

Retreat past the inner wall (Go to **116**)

The road through the inner gate, the path to safety, is roiling with bodies.

It looks like the evacuation of the populace is taking longer than expected. The soldiers on the front line will do all they can to continue the fight until the evacuation is complete, but if they can't make it…

There's a tremor from far away, a periodic rumble.

Titan footsteps. And not far apart. It's running.

"It's a Titan!"

"It's right over there!"

A Titan is running straight for you along the broad main street from the gate.

The crowd is gripped by panic.

A Titan of more than ten meters tall at a run can reach quite a pace. Soldiers pursue it with vertical maneuvering to defend, but no one can catch it.

It must have come barreling past both the front and middle guards. It's an Abnormal.

The Titan, a smile on its face, leans over and dashes for the assembled evacuees. Cries of despair run through the crowd.

Then suddenly…

You see a human form career through the air behind the Titan. It's Mikasa, using her vertical maneuvering equipment.

She slips through the air as if she really can fly, and soon catches up with the Titan.

As she leaps, she sets an anchor in the running monster. Picking up speed, she reaches its neck and sinks her blades into its nape.

With a crash, the Titan falls.

Its head lands only steps from the crowd of evacuees.

She was just in the nick of time.

Still, you can only admire Mikasa's talent. You've never seen anyone move like that.

She always excelled during training, but how can she acquit herself like this in her very first battle with real Titans?

Mikasa, for her part, jumps down to the ground with her usual bland expression, as if nothing special has happened. (Go to **93**)

•85

Urban warfare against Titans is an ugly thing. It doesn't go like it did in training. Titans who fight back are far more terrifying than you had imagined.

First one person, then another, falls to the monsters: other soldiers, classmates whose names you hardly know. With each one, Krista begins to weep afresh.

She moves to face the Titans and protect your comrades, heedless of her own safety.

You…

Risk your own life to protect her (Go to **238**)

Hold her back and tell her not to do anything rash (Go to **286**)

•86

With Eren in your arms, you use vertical maneuvering to head for the rear.

You pause on a rooftop to bind the stump of his leg and stanch the bleeding. Eren groans, tears in his eyes. He must be in terrible pain, but you assume that isn't what makes him cry out.

You pick him up again. You have no words to say to him. It's all you can do to work the maneuvering equipment with two people's weight.

(Record that Eren has been wounded, and **mark Armin Arlert dead**. Go to **112**.)

You've heard terrible news from a member of another squad: headquarters has been surrounded by Titans, making it impossible to get any more gas for your vertical maneuvering equipment.

The vertical maneuvering equipment allows a person to move at high speed using only a small machine; and to do so it requires pressurized gas, which it consumes at a high rate. Because of the hopeless battle you fought after the order to advance, your squad is nearly out of propellant. Even if you're careful to conserve it, you're not sure how long you can last...

The rooftops around the headquarters building are populated with fellow soldiers who came here to be resupplied. Now they stand in shock. Things look bleak.

Jean sits down on the roof and sighs. "What a stupid life I had... If I'd known it was going to end this way, I would've just said something..." You don't know what he's talking about, but he lapses into silence.

Marco stands not far away. "This is awful," he mutters. "I was ready to die, but...I'd hoped I would know what I was dying for..."

Reiner, Bertolt, and Annie are all close by. They're talking about how to handle the situation. But as skilled as they are, without gas even they are helpless...

Everywhere you see your despairing brothers and sisters in arms. Sitting among them is Armin. (Go to **124**)

Heedless of your own safety, you launch yourself at the Titan.

It spits out Thomas, whom it was about to eat; the lower half of his body is covered in Titan saliva, but he's alive.

"Everyone, stay calm and do what we learned in training!" Eren says courageously.

"There's another one down below. Be careful!"

"The small ones can be quick. Set your wires so you can strike and get away in one go."

Everyone in Squad 34 takes a breath, then works together to bring down the Titans.

"We did it!" Eren exclaims joyously.

Everyone cheers. Your first victory in a real battle!

But Armin says quietly, "Real combat isn't like training at all. The sight and sound of a living Titan is something else. If any of us had made a single wrong move, we might all be dead now."

Thomas groans; his leg has been hurt.

Armin's right: you can't get too carried away.

"Let's take Thomas and fall back. We have to report that the front-line troops have been decimated, too."

Squad 34, all its members alive, heads for the rear.

Now you…

Join the middle group's defensive action and continue the fight

(Go to 297)

Take the wounded Thomas and withdraw through the inner gate

(Go to 90)

•89

You hear a bell ring out, clang, clang, clang, announcing that the populace has been evacuated. It's also the signal for the soldiers to retreat. Your duty today is finally over. You can fall back to safety…

Then you notice a trainee, a young woman with black hair, coming your way.

Armin calls out: "Mikasa!"

In a single, fluid movement, Mikasa lands next to you.

"Hey, Mikasa!" Eren says loudly. "I wish you could've seen my first battle! I'll bet you did pretty well yourself, but the Titan I took down was—"

Mikasa ignores what he's saying and catches him up in a hug.

"I'm so glad you're alive." (Go to **281**)

You withdraw, taking the injured Thomas with you.

You make for the headquarters building, but are informed that headquarters functions have been moved rearward, inside the inner gate. That's also the best place to get treatment for the wounded.

You split off from the rest of Squad 34 and head for the inner gate.

On the other side, the gate is more packed with evacuees and Garrison soldiers than you expected.

Not all the squads have been as lucky as yours. You see badly-wounded soldiers, and hear reports of a battle not going in humanity's favor.

You find a field hospital, but they tell you Thomas's injury is nothing, and to take him elsewhere. You're moved on from place after place. At last you find a first-aid center with some space. By the time you get Thomas settled there, a great deal of time has passed.

Clang, clang, clang! You hear a bell ring out. The evacuation is finished, and the soldiers are being ordered to retreat.

Are the others from Squad 34 still safe?

From among the crowd, someone says to you, "So you guys made it out, too?" It's your fellow trainee, Krista. She's come here with a wounded squadmate of her own. (Go to **252**)

●91

You, Krista, and the others withdraw beyond the inner wall.

The far side of the wall is overflowing with evacuated soldiers and citizens. (Go to **237**)

●92

You add your voice to Krista's.

Perhaps moved by your pleas, the soldier nods and says, "I can understand how you feel. I'll notify the defense squadron commander."

Phew. You and Krista smile at each other.

But…after the soldier leaves, the freckled girl gets a sour expression on her face and says, "Not gonna happen. He won't notify a damn person. And even if he did, we'd never get permission."

This seems like a bit much even for someone who's known for her bad attitude. Krista looks disappointed, too.

But she's right. No matter how long you wait, no help comes.

You try to ask several more times, but you are turned away with only a harsh word.

(Increase your Affinity with Krista by 1 and go to 144.)

A greedy merchant has blocked the inner gate with a cart loaded down with goods.

The gate is too small for the cart to pass through, but the merchant insists on trying to push it through anyway.

So this is why the evacuation is taking so long.

The merchant and some of his flunkies are trying to control the crowd.

"That cargo is worth more than all of you together could earn in a lifetime! Lend aid, and you'll be rewarded!"

What a self-serving thing to say when you've blocked off the only escape route, putting people's lives at risk! This merchant is powerful enough that he's even got pull with the army; soldiers stand by helplessly.

Then, Mikasa arrives.

For an instant her eyes go wide, but she quickly returns to her usual flat expression.

"My comrades are dying as you speak," she says. "They are dying holding off the Titans, to buy enough time for the evacuation."

The merchant spits back, "Of course they are! Give yourselves for the lives and the property of the populace—that's your duty as a soldier, isn't it?"

Mikasa takes a step closer to the merchant, sword in hand, expression unchanging.

"If you think it is so obvious that one person should die for another, then surely you'll understand…how the loss of your single, precious life may be forgiven in the interest of saving so many others."

You…

Stand and watch (Go to **68**)

Take Mikasa's side. A guy like this deserves to die (Go to **158**)

Take the merchant's side (Go to **291**)

Jump in between Mikasa and the merchant and try to think of something… Look carefully at this page.

You make a dash for the remaining cannon. A lone soldier is working it, his face covered in soot and sweat and fear.

"Thanks, trainee. Help me load 'er up!"

You load a cannonball into the gun, which is still so hot you fear you'll get burned.

The soldier fires the cannon. There's an ear-splitting roar, and the cannonball rips into the leg of a Titan advancing toward you.

The soldier whoops and throws up his arms. "Take that, you damn monster!"

An instant later, though, a piece of debris kicked by another Titan comes flying through the air. You throw yourself to the ground.

When you look back at the soldier, you see everything but his head.

For the Titan, it had probably been like kicking a pebble. But humans are fragile things.

You look forward again. The destroyed leg of the Titan in front of you is regenerating in a cloud of steam.

You…

Take over the cannon from the dead soldier (go to **261**)

Ascend the wall (go to **65**)

Run like hell (go to **136**)

Before you can say a word, the one-legged Eren speaks in a strained voice.

"Everyone's...dead... Even Armin... It...It should've been me... Armin was the one...who told me about the outside world...if it weren't for him, I would've..."

Mikasa's expression never changes, but she says, "This is no time to be getting sentimental."

She turns that same expressionless face to you. "Are you the one who saved Eren?"

You nod, and she says simply, "Please take care of him a little longer. I'll back you up."

(Increase your **Affinity with Mikasa** by 1 and go to **242**.)

●96

You've made your way back up the wall using vertical maneuvering. You collect your scattered wits and look around.

It looks like everyone is all right. One trainee is unconscious, but Sasha is already setting her anchors and rescuing him.

At that moment, a vast rumble threatens to turn heaven and earth upside-down, and the wall shakes violently.

Chips fly up from directly below you—the gate has been pulverized!

It's the Colossus Titan. The one that appeared suddenly in Shiganshina District and destroyed the wall there five years ago.

You've only heard stories—but now it seems to be happening again right in front of you!

You hear your companions yelling—and screaming.

You hear another explosion, this time from atop the wall, and see more fragments fly into the air in a cloud of smoke. Cannon barrels rocket into the sky like so much confetti. (Go to **56**)

●97

Sasha immediately jumps down the wall to help your unconscious comrade. She's used one of the two guide wires of her vertical maneuvering equipment to stop his fall, and you doubt if a single wire can support the weight of two people. You rush down the wall to help. Samuel, the boy you've rescued, is injured, but alive. **(Increase your Affinity with Sasha by 1 and go to 104.)**

•98

You and the others move to provide relief and extract your comrades still in the city.

More and more Titans are wandering the streets.

Injuries and casualties for both the rescued and the rescuers are hardly negligible…but still, you were able to save quite a few of your friends.

You notice Eren among those you rescued. He thanks you:

"I'm glad you came. Now we can strike back against those Titans!" (Go to **213**)

•99

You have to protect something as pure as her.

You agree with Krista, and plan to guard her with all your strength. You think people's morale will go up just by having her in charge. You tell her as much, as you say you're joining her command.

"B-But I would hate for you to get hurt," she says. That perfect smile again. You would gladly give your life for her.

The freckled girl harumphs, but doesn't say anything.

(Increase your Affinity with Krista by 1 and go to 85.)

WN UHII OI OD DNH DN
ƎWUN ꓤIƎHI DDH SNHIII
ꓓIꓒIIINW ꓤꓤH ƎꓤƎHI II

•100 – Titan Panorama

It's your fearsome ene-mies—the Titans. Take a close look.

If you can observe calmly even in the heat of battle, you may find a key to victory.

(When you are done study-ing this section, return to the section you were at before. If you can't figure it out, start over from **60**. You may con-sult this section at any time. When battling the Titans, you may be told that you may look at **100**. In that event, mark your page with a bookmark or finger and turn to this section.)

The ground forces are already nearly annihilated. The mobile guns deployed near the gate have been kicked apart by Titans.

Occasionally a cannonball from the fixed emplacements on the wall flies over your head. The walltop guns were intended to fire outward—but with Titans running amok in the city, the only choice was to spin the guns around.

You glance around, but see no other soldiers using vertical maneuvering nearby.

Normally, the fixed guns use grapeshot to slow the Titans, after which elite soldiers finish them off with the help of vertical maneuvering equipment. Normally. That's what they taught you in training.

But you gather all the soldiers involved in that strategy are gone.

On the ground you see the corpse of a soldier, lying on its side, a sword in its hand.

Now, what do you do?

Other than the wall, there are few buildings in the immediate vicinity, making it hard for an inexperienced hand to fight the Titans.

Trust the gunners and focus on felling the Titans (Go to 155)

Fight the Titans while dodging cannonballs (Go to 120)

Give up and ascend the wall (Go to 280)

"We have to help the townspeople—and our friends!" Krista says. "B-But I don't want everyone here to be put in danger!"

Even here, on the battlefield, she sounds like an angel.

The hard-eyed freckly girl is there, of course. She snorts and says, "Nice talk, but not practical. You always were an idealist, Krista."

Maybe it would be better to trust Jean with the command (go to **140**) or Marco (go to **66**). If you decide to give Krista the command anyway, go to **79**.

●103

"…You're right." Mikasa nods firmly. "Eren promised me. Promised he wouldn't die."

She seems to have regained her composure. (Increase your **Affinity with Mikasa** by 1 and go to **84**.)

●104

Suddenly there's a roar like a volcanic eruption, and the area is filled with hot steam.

Everything goes white; you can hardly see. (Go to **59**)

●105

You help organize and direct the evacuation, but it seems to be going too slowly.

Part of it is the suddenness of the Titan attack, but…it looks like there's a cart blocking the escape route. People are milling about near the road through the inner wall. It's chaos.

From far off you hear a shout: "It's an Abnormal!"

You see a Titan coming down the main street toward your position at a terrible speed.

Veteran Garrison soldiers rush to respond, but the Titan is quicker than they are. It kicks at the ones who have floated into the air with their vertical maneuvering equipment, or simply runs past them.

The Titan dives into the crowd of evacuees.

There's a sound of something breaking, and then a chorus of screams.

You see people fly into the air.

Rubble, debris, and human bodies tumble toward you— (Go to **145**)

Two streets up, you see a Titan running at high speed. An Abnormal.

"The evacuees are that way!"

But Jean replies in a quavering voice, "Don't go. The evacuation must be finished by now. And if it isn't, the elite soldiers are protecting the rear." (Go to **267**)

Before you can speak, Armin says in a strained voice, "Those five carried out their mission…and died bravely in battle…"

You think there must be a better way to tell an old friend about the death of someone to whom she was so close, but you can't imagine what it might be.

The other trainees, learning of this turn for the first time, cry out. But Mikasa is strangely calm. She says only, "This is no time to be getting sentimental."

You can't guess what she may be thinking.

But she's right. (Go to **117**)

•108

But…

You see a signal flare rise up from the city.

Red smoke. Something terrible has happened, or the plan has been aborted.

What in the world is going on?

At length, you observe a change in the behavior of the clustered Titans. Several of them begin walking toward the city, as if drawn by something.

They're heading for the boulder…where Eren and the picked troops are staging their plan.

You…

Take some of the gas tanks and head for Eren's position (Go to **205**)

Descend into the city and fight the departing Titans (Go to **212**)

See your duty through at your current position (Go to **187**)

•109

You join the soldiers firing the cannons. You shoot and shoot, knowing you won't stop the Titan invasion, knowing you can't help your fellow soldiers on the ground—with only the faith that it will be of some small use… (Go to **63**)

●110

You stand by with Jean and the others.

Rumors are running wild among your comrades: Eren turned into a Titan. He was eaten by a Titan. He was eaten by a Titan that then turned into him...

You were told to stand by, but you can't shake the sense the Garrison soldiers all around are watching you. Does this have something to do with what happened to Eren? (Go to **258**)

●111

The plan...is a success.

It was a close call. During the assault, only five of the seven Titans were killed.

It's no one's fault—it was a risky plan to begin with. But it was Mikasa and Annie who brought down the last two.

With no help from vertical maneuvering equipment, only their own strength, they'd leapt three meters into the air to kill those Titans. Incredible.

Thanks to the two women, the plan has miraculously come off. (Go to **226**)

Someone on the ground is shouting. It's Hannah.

You settle to the earth.

"Franz isn't breathing. Help him!"

Weeping, she presses on his chest with all her strength, trying to bring him back to life.

You take in the scene with a sense of unreality.

The entire lower half of Franz's body is gone. He's obviously already dead.

You…

Have no time for this. You leave the scene (Go to **221**)

Try to revive Franz (Go to **154**)

Drag Hannah away (Go to **181**)

You make for the soldiers' position once the Titans have left.

Someone is on the ground, shouting. It's your classmate, Hannah.

"Help Franz!" she cries as you land.

Franz is just nearby…the top half of him is, anyway. And it's not moving.

"It's no use. He's long gone," the freckled girl says.

Krista's face twists and she begins to cry.

Hannah lets out one gasping sob after another, unwilling to give up on Franz—but you and the others push her off the body and drag her away. It's for her own safety. She can't be here, alone, in this state.

(**Mark Franz Kefka dead** and go to **80**.)

•114

It is a terrible plan, one likely to claim a great many lives. And yet—some may survive.

Do you tell the others about the plan?

Think of another way (go to **139**)

Do things this way (go to **173**)

"Squad 34, move out!"

Eren gives the order, and the whole squad moves.

Using your vertical maneuvering equipment, you jump from rooftop to rooftop. With each jump you reel your wires in, set a new anchor, then reel them in again, picking up speed each time. The wind whips around you, howling in your ears, as the reddish rooftops rush past.

In between the buildings ahead, you see swaying humanoid silhouettes, a great many of them.

It's the Titans. They're already past the middle guard!

"The Titans have come this far already?!"

"What happened to the vanguard?"

The experienced Garrison soldiers up front were supposed to stop the Titans. That was the plan.

And you were supposed to join the battle straight away.

The battle has barely started, and it looks like the vanguard has already been shattered... (go to **217**)

●116

You know how Mikasa feels, and you have no intention of stopping her.

You'd probably just be a burden if you tried to go with her, though...

You and the soldiers of the Garrison retreat past the wall. (Go to **170**)

Mikasa raises her sword above her head and proclaims, "If we can clear out the Titans swarming the headquarters, we can get enough gas for everyone to make it onto the wall."

But the others aren't convinced: "How will we take on that many Titans…?"

"I can do it. Even if I have to do it myself. I am strong. And you… you're cowards. You mewling kittens can sit here and watch me."

Her expression never changes as she speaks. She seems to be trying to goad the others to action, but she's not doing a very good job.

"If I fail, I'll die… But if I win, I'll live."

Her words may be blunt, but they're true. Everyone there seems to realize it.

"And if we don't fight, we can't win."

Without waiting for a response, she flies off in the direction of Headquarters.

Jean mutters something, then rises to follow her.

"Hey! Were we taught to let one of our own fight alone?!"

The words seem to decide everyone. One after another they leap after Jean and Mikasa. You…

Follow Mikasa (go to **199**)

Follow Jean (go to **253**)

You stand between them and offer your idea:

Even the merchant can see the cart will never get through the tunnel. Why not have people carry the cargo through by hand, even just some of it? What can't be carried could be stashed in a spot unlikely to be attacked by Titans. Since Titans only attack humans, if the cargo were stored in a basement or other safe place, there would be a good chance of coming back to get it later…wouldn't there?

"Collect it later? If Trost District falls to the Titans, it would be lost to me!" The merchant scrunches up his face, but after a moment he seems to start thinking like a businessman again, calculating. Finally, he nods. "Fine. Far be it from the merchant Dimo Reeves to put his own property above the safety of the populace. I'm sure you'll let everyone know what you've seen here."

He starts issuing orders to his cronies. "Pull the cart back! Those with the Merchants' Association, take as much cargo as you can carry!"

The townspeople cheer. With the road cleared, the evacuation resumes.

There are taunting voices: "So are you soldiers the pets of a few greedy businessman?" But mostly you hear words of gratitude.

"As a show of gratitude, I'll let you in on a little something," Dimo says. "I left a delivery horse loaded with goods for the Garrison at the Merchants' Association building. I knew as well as you do that the Titans don't attack non-human animals, and I gambled that it would survive. If it's still there, it's in a barn near the building. There's every chance the horse and all its supplies are gone, though—you're welcome to have a look yourself."

He wears a cunning look and an incongruous smile. "If the animal is there, I want you to report to the Garrison that Reeves the merchant provided them with supplies in their hour of need. I fully expect to collect a reward."

Unlike the average pack horse, the horses that supply the Garrison are of exceptional pedigree and training. They do not quail even at the sight of a Titan, and have superb stamina. Back when you were being trained with the horses, you remember being told one of these animals was worth as much as a human life.

You commit the location to memory and plan to make use of the animal if you have the chance and the need.

(From this point on, when you see the words "If you have/had a horse," you may add **6** to the section number and go to that section. Remember this or make a note of it. Go to **83**.)

You are assigned to the rear group.

This is supposed to be the last line of defense. If the Titans get past the front and middle guards, it will be your job to protect the evacuating citizens and make sure the Titans do not break through Wall Rose. Veteran soldiers of the Garrison are with you.

You might have been picked for this assignment because of your superior ability—or it might just be they didn't think you could do any good up at the front. Either way, you'd best help with the evacuation…

You look up and see Mikasa. Looks like she's been assigned to the rear, as well. In the 104th Training Corps, she was the crème de la crème. It's only natural she would be stationed here. You're relieved to be near her.

But…something's off. Her usual calm demeanor is gone; she seems skittish. (Go to **81**)

The cannonballs are even faster than you are with your vertical maneuvering equipment. Still, you try to fight while dodging the cannon fire—but the Titans aren't that stupid.

As you struggle to maneuver, a massive hand grabs you out of the air.

The Titan is struck by several cannonballs, taking off half its head, but it's already regenerating in a cloud of steam. Then it opens its huge mouth and swallows you whole. (Go to **14**)

●121

Your comrades in Squad 34 bravely face down the seven-meter Titan that has appeared.

They fire the wires of their vertical maneuvering equipment into the monster as they leap from the buildings and move to strike.

"We've got to help Eren!"

But the Titan sweeps away the wires with its arm. Your friends miss their mark, or go flying into walls. (Go to 132)

●122

The female soldier with the glasses says to you:

"There's no point talking to you if you can't even make a calculation like that. It's not like the rest of us are watching our comrades die just for fun."

And she leaves. (Go to 144)

The ground level has become a hellscape.

Titans pour in through the huge hole in front of you.

You see the ruins of wheeled cannons and supply wagons. The mobile ground cannons never were as powerful as the fixed emplacements on the wall.

Most likely, the ground crews were supposed to use the big guns to take out the Titans, supported by fire from the wall, while they used the materials in the wagons to plug the hole. You're sure they must have practiced it many times. But no battle plan survives contact with the Titans.

Smoke and explosions whirl around you. Now and again, you can hear a faint voice among them. The neighing of horses. And the screams of people being eaten by Titans.

You…

Make for the cannon and help with firing (Go to **94**)

Fight the Titans on horseback (Go to **141**)

Try to help the wounded (Go to **182**)

You are standing on a building tall enough to see out over Trost District.

The surviving members of the 104th Training Corps surround you.

Many have gone limp with despair—with the scale of the destruction and the deaths of their friends, and more, with the knowledge that Headquarters has been surrounded and the supply of gas cut off.

A bell rings: *clang, clang, clang*. That's the signal that the evacuation is complete. It's also the order for all soldiers to retreat. At last, you have fulfilled your duty. You can fall back to safety…

You can't escape the irony that the retreat order should be issued now. Ascending the wall takes more gas than actual combat. With your remaining supply, you can't hope to withdraw.

Then you notice a trainee with black hair coming toward you through the sky. It's Mikasa.

She lands near you in a single, fluid movement.

"Where's the rest of Squad 34?" she asks.

Check your Battle Record Sheet.

Armin is dead (Go to **95**)

Eren is dead (Go to **107**)

Armin and Eren are both dead (Go to **244**)

"We can't let everyone endanger themselves! I'll be the decoy," Eren shouts, jumping up.

He says he'll collect everyone's remaining gas, then go out and distract the Titans. As long as he's just running up to the roof, and not trying to fight, the modicum of gas should see him through.

His plan is terrifyingly dangerous…but not without merit.

"I'm going with you," Mikasa says, rising.

Jean and several others raise their voices, inspired by the pair's determination.

This decoy idea is a thin hope…but it's hope.

If nothing else, the air in the room has changed. You have a plan. (Go to **266**)

●126

A relief mission gets underway, organized by the veterans of the Garrison.

You and the other trainees request to be part of the effort.

Check your casualty list.

Eren Yeager is alive (Go to **98**)

Eren Yeager is dead (Go to **204**)

●127

Check your Battle Record Sheet. Is Marco Bott still alive?

Marco is alive (Go to **243**)

Marco is dead (Go to **249**)

The ones you rescued were Franz and Hannah.

They hold each other jubilantly.

"You were so brave, Franz, shielding me like that…"

"I just wanted to save you. That's all."

You can't pry them apart. And you're pretty sure it was you and your friends who saved both of them…

But then, they've been lovebirds since training—and in the midst of a battle rife with cruelty, to see them warms your heart.

"Geez," someone mutters lightly, "we should've left you there." (Go to **67**)

You make a snap decision to support Eren. Your feet pound against the wall as you run in the opposite direction from him.

The huge eyes roll in the huge face to leer down at you. If you can get the thing's attention, maybe that will help Eren.

The Titan raises a massive, steam-clouded hand. You throw yourself from the top of the wall and run down the side. You fire your vertical maneuvering equipment's anchors into the side of the wall. (Go to **104**)

●130

Sasha agrees eagerly with your suggestion:

"Food! Great idea. Times like this, you need a good meal!"

You search the area and discover some provisions. Of course Headquarters would have emergency stores. You even find some meat, perhaps intended for the commanders. You and Sasha put it on plates and pass everyone a share.

But not many find themselves able to eat. As they put the food in their mouths, some seem haunted by the memory of Titans eating their friends.

You don't have much appetite, either. But you force yourself to eat, chew, swallow.

It helps revitalize you, just a little. Your head starts to clear.

You're not sure what the best plan is, but you know action is better than sitting still. You've got some capable companions—they'll be able to figure something out.

(Increase your **Affinity with Sasha** by 1, then go to **139** and consider another plan.)

●**131**

"Go back, damn you! Mikasa's still—"

Eren shouts and struggles violently in your arms.

Selfish man. He has no idea how she feels.

"Stop! Stop it!" His cries turn from anger to a howl of grief.

"Wasn't Armin enough? Not Mikasa, too— Curse me…!"

It hurts your heart—but you refuse to let it show on your face. You pick up speed with your vertical maneuvering equipment.

At that instant, you're slammed by some impact, flung through the air.

Is Eren struggling again? No, this was much too powerful…

A Titan, then—?!

You quickly right yourself, then roll along a rooftop, shedding speed. (Go to **175**)

A scene of surpassing horror unfolds before your eyes.

A big-headed seven-meter Titan pulls one of your comrades close by the wires of his gear and grabs him.

Nac and Mylius, unable to make use of their vertical maneuvering equipment, die screaming in the mouths of Titans.

Mina, the girl who collided with the wall, is on the ground, motionless.

Another Titan approaches. It has black hair and googly eyes. Just three or four meters tall, it stuffs Mina into its mouth head first. As Titans go, it's small. If her maneuvering gear were operational, she might well have been able to defeat it based on her training.

Everyone had been so ready for battle just moments ago, and now… this. Who knew how different training was from real combat? This is a nightmare. It has to be.

(Mark Squad 34 dead. Thomas Wagner, Mina Carolina, Nac Tius, and Mylius Zeramuski are all dead. Go to **133.**)

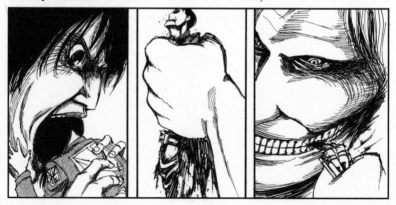

Eren is lying prone. One of his legs is gone. Is he even still alive?

Armin appears to be in one piece, but he stares vacantly into space, eyes wide.

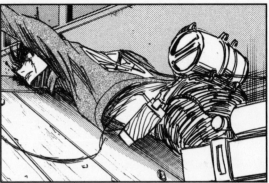

Yet another Titan appears. Taller than the rooftops, with an old man's face and a long beard. Its eyes are narrowed, its mouth half-open. It plucks Armin off the rooftop and carries him toward its mouth…

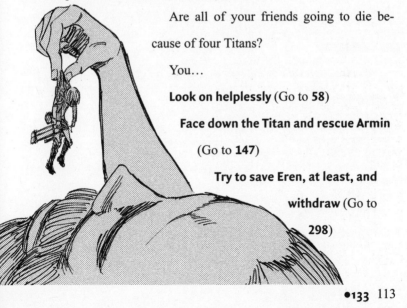

Are all of your friends going to die because of four Titans?

You…

Look on helplessly (Go to **58**)

Face down the Titan and rescue Armin (Go to **147**)

Try to save Eren, at least, and withdraw (Go to **298**)

A defensive regiment is formed with three elite soldiers of the Garrison—Ian Dietrich, Mitabi Jarnach, and Rico Brzenska—each heading a squadron.

You and Mikasa are assigned under them. It's dangerous work, but you were given it because you're close to Eren.

The other soldiers have succeeded, at great cost, in drawing the Titans in the city into one spot.

This operation hinges on you and your companions, and it's almost time to begin.

Eren and his guard unit—that is, you—descend into the city with vertical maneuvering. The streets are empty of humans and Titans alike, and you move along as quickly as you can.

You see your goal, the boulder. Eren catapults into the air and bites his own hand.

An explosion sounds above you; smoke billows everywhere. A Titan appears before your eyes.

You and the rest of the guard unit take up positions on the surrounding rooftops, and prepare to defend it. (Go to **268**)

•135

You give your answer.

"The boulder? I see," Pixis says, and nods as in agreement. (Go to **193**)

•136

Nearly insane with terror, you flee. You grip the controls of your vertical maneuvering equipment, but your hands are shaking so badly you have trouble using them.

You trip on a torn-up piece of flagstone and fall. A giant hand surrounds you, lifts you into the air.

You're still screaming in horror as the Titan bites down. (Go to **14**)

•137

"…That's how things stand," Armin says. "If all we need to do is clear out the three-to-four-meter ones from the houses, there might be another way."

He might be mad with grief over Eren…or he might have had the same thought you did.

"It's not any safer. But if it works, we could save everybody."

And he begins to explain. (Go to **166**)

•138

Completely focused, you fly toward the Titan, deliver a cut to its face.

You'd had hopes of getting it to spit out Thomas. But in the next second, it turns toward you and bites down.

The last thing you hear is a great gulp as it swallows you. (Go to **14**)

You're inside the headquarters building.

All the surviving members of the 104th Training Corps are gathered here.

At the moment, the building is surrounded by several Titans of approximately 15 meters each. The building is sturdy and they won't soon break it down, but so long as there are humans here, more Titans will come.

Furthermore, everyone is effectively out of gas, and so unable to fight with vertical maneuvering.

Gas supplies are on the first floor, but so is a group of relatively small, three-to-four-meter Titans. Reconnaissance suggested there were seven of them total. If you can't get rid of them, you'll have to go without gas.

There has to be a way to break this impasse.

"The situation is hopeless anyway, so no idea is too outrageous to consider. Everyone, think of anything you can."

What kind of plan do you propose?

Stay sequestered in here (Go to 156)

Start with some food (Go to 130)

Use one or more people as bait while another group grabs the gas canisters (Go to 114)

If Armin Arlert is alive, you may also make the following choices:

Follow Armin's plan (Go to 275)

Confuse the Titans by sending Armin out in drag (Go to 151)

"Feh. Fine. You, come on."

Jean maneuvers to the top of the highest building in the vicinity. He was one of the best at vertical maneuvering in training, and you can see the results on the battlefield.

"Keep an eye on the situation from here. Make sure you see any Titan movement."

Jean surveys the area calmly, making no move to go himself.

In the distance, you can see the Garrison soldiers fighting a pitched battle. Your companions are shouting that you have to help them, but Jean says stoically:

"Even the experienced soldiers are hard-pressed. What could a bunch of greenhorns do? Pay attention to the field. If a Titan comes for us, we run. If we can't run, then we fight. No need for us to die sooner than we have to."

His words are cold, but he's right. Jean's voice quavers as he speaks— he doesn't like abandoning the others any more than you do.

Still, you're surprised.

You would've expected Jean to be far more insufferable in a command role...

(Increase your **Affinity with Jean** by 1 and go to **106**.)

●141

You were trained to ride in boot camp, and you consider fighting from horseback.

However, most of the horses that were here have run away, and the rest are neighing in terror.

Try to ride one of them anyway (Go to **248**)

Give up and help with the cannon (Go to **94**)

Ascend the wall (Go to **65**)

●142

You and your surviving comrades join the middle guard.

The Titans are relentless, but you face them down. Even the scant experience you've had in the battle so far is proving valuable.

Your classmates are falling. Experienced soldiers are falling. And amidst it all, you're fighting for your life against a massive Titan.

You wonder how much time has passed… (Go to **171**)

●143

The battle for Trost District is not looking good.

The dead are piling up—the soldiers of the Garrison as well as your fellow trainees.

This is, after all, your first encounter with actual Titans. Training and exercises are well and good, but an actual Titan is a far more terrible thing than you could have prepared for.

You and the others zip around the battlefield, dodging Titans, stopping to help the fallen when you see them.

In a way, it's worse than actual combat. Most of those you find are dead, their bodies torn, shattered.

The ones who aren't, though, you can rarely save—they simply die moaning before your eyes.

Krista struggles to save them.

She offers them encouragement in her beautiful voice, holding their blood-soaked hands.

You credit the sight of her for helping you retain some shred of sanity.

Because so far, out of all those you've encountered, you haven't managed to help a single one. (Go to **198**)

●144

With no relief effort to be mounted, you can only wait.

Krista continues to pray fervently for your friends' safe return. (Go to **186**)

When you come to, you're lying on your side in a bed.

By some miracle, you seem to have been saved. Maybe you were pulled from the rubble.

"You're awake, trainee?"

A stranger in a soldier's uniform sits beside you.

You hurry to face him.

What happened after...that? First things first...you need to know what happened to Mikasa. You ask the man.

"Mikasa Ackerman is safe. As is Eren Yeager, whom she rescued. I've been told Trainee Eren was about to be eaten alive when she appeared."

Thank God. Mikasa was able to do what she'd set out to do...

But the man continues matter-of-factly.

He tells you the evacuation of Trost District failed, and the populace was decimated. Wall Rose was abandoned. Humanity's territory has been reduced to the all-too-confined boundaries of Wall Sheena...

You notice the crest on the man's uniform. He's with the Military Police Brigade.

"Trainees Eren and Mikasa will be court-martialed. We'll need you to testify," he says with disinterest, and then he says nothing more.

(Bad Ending – The Trial of Eren and Mikasa)

You ask if there's any way to get word to the Survey Corps outside the wall.

"No," a more experienced soldier says with a strained expression. Then he goes on:

"They purposely set up no way to get word to them. Once the Survey Corps is outside the wall, their commanders don't want any interference.

"It's a political problem. There's a very vocal faction that wants to do away with surveys of the world outside the wall. If it were too easy to call the Corps back for, say, a rescue mission, there are those who would use that capability to interfere with their activities.

"Damn those politicians. It's their fault that at a crucial time like this, we can't…"

What a terrible state of affairs. And you can't even blame the Titans; humans did this to themselves.

But at the same time, you realize something. Just because there's no system, doesn't mean it's impossible.

Go back to **72** and take careful stock of the scene. There must be some answer.

You advance toward the Titan. Utterly focused, you shove Armin out of the way. But the Titan snatches you instead, tossing you into its massive jaws. You land on its huge tongue. Without a moment's mercy, the

Titan closes its mouth.

You managed to save your friend…but not yourself. (Go to **14**.)

●148

You suggest that rather than fighting the Titans directly, it might be better to give support where you can.

There may be survivors among the units decimated by the Titans. If you avoid direct confrontation, you might be able to save some of them…

"That's a wonderful idea!"

Krista agrees with you eagerly, her eyes shining.

"Yeah, that's not half bad," says the freckled girl, there as always, with a crooked smile on her face. "We stay safe, and we get the satisfaction of helping our comrades."

She always has to add a little twist of the knife…

You break off from Jean and the others, and start working.

(Increase your **Affinity with Krista** by **1**, and go to **143**.)

●149

You understand how Mikasa feels. You're worried about your friends, too.

With a burst of gas from your vertical maneuvering equipment, you set off after her.

There's always a risk you'll just be a burden, but you might also be able to help your friends. (Go to **69**)

•150

"All right. Leave it to me. Just buy me a little time."

Armin seems to have an idea. You've decided to trust him.

And then, to protect him and Eren, you throw yourself into battle with the Titans.

(Increase your **Affinity with Armin** by **2**, and go to **276**.)

•151

"All right. If it'll help us, I'll…I'll give it a try."

You pass Armin the woman's dress you happen to have found.

In his new outfit, Armin looks strikingly like a beautiful young woman. He's almost as pretty as Krista.

"N-Now what do I do?" Armin asks, and you give a start.

Honestly, you hadn't thought that far.

When you stop and think, you realize Titans will attack any human, and it probably won't make much difference whether or not they're wearing a soldier's uniform. You admit your mistake and apologize.

"Damn you!" Jean yells at you. "Playing games at a time like this!"

But you see a lot of smiles.

"You've got to be kidding me."

One of the trainee girls is laughing so hard she's crying. "How can a boy look that good in a dress? You're putting me to shame!"

"Darn it! If we get out of this alive, I'll show you just how pretty I can be!"

Your friends, weighed down by despair just a moment ago, are bantering together.

Even Armin is laughing.

Your "plan" has helped lighten the mood—even if that wasn't what you intended.

After a good laugh, Armin says with a relaxed look, "You know, I think that helped me calm down. And I've thought of a plan. Listen."

(Go to **275**)

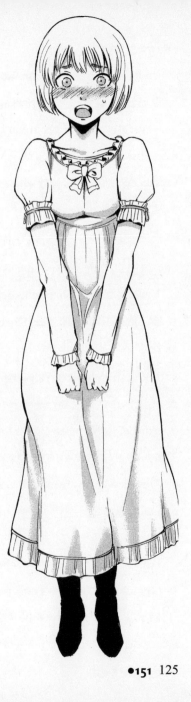

●**152**

You watch Eren as he flies at the Colossus Titan. Its body is like a wall, and he sinks his anchors into the Titan itself, using them to aid his vertical maneuvering. He didn't learn that in training. You can only marvel at his flying. He looks like a speck against the Colossus Titan, but exactly because he is so small, it's not easy for the Titan to react quickly to him. Eren lets his guide wires out, describing a wide arc. He's behind the Colossus Titan! Now all he has to do is strike its nape... (go to **104**)

●**153**

You shout for Eren to calm down.

But in his frenzy, it's as if he doesn't hear you... (go to **180**)

●**154**

You start trying to revive Franz.

It's obvious he's already gone. This is for Hannah's sake.

You cradle his head to clear the airway, just like you learned training. Then you press down on his chest.

Franz's face is already growing cold, but his expression is somehow peaceful. Perhaps it's because he died saving the person he loved.

"It's all right."

Hannah's voice comes from behind you.

"It's all right, I get it. Franz is... He's dead."

She can barely squeeze the words out. You offer her what encouragement you can, then fire up your vertical maneuvering equipment and leave the scene.

(**Mark Franz Kefka dead** and go to **142**.)

●155

This is a wiser decision than trying to focus on two things at once.

As soon as one barrage has cleared your head, you steel your resolve and throw yourself at the Titans.

Luckily, no cannonballs come flying at you. From overhead, you hear something like a cheer. It seems the soldiers on the wall have noticed you.

You focus on one Titan whose movement has been hampered by the barrage and maneuver behind it. You draw your blade in midair, throw your speed and weight into the nape of its neck, make the cut, and kill it.

Just like in training. From the corner of your eye you see the Titan collapse in a cloud of steam.

But you are snatched from the air by a giant hand.

Other Titans swarm you, tear you limb from limb.

You succeeded in striking a blow, yes, but there are just too many of them. (Go to **14**)

The headquarters building is solidly built, and stocked with provisions and water. Why not just stay there, you ask. As long as you take deal with the little Titans, and the hands of the bigger ones that reach into the fissures in the building, you should have a better chance of surviving than if you do anything rash.

Mikasa is immediately opposed: "The Titans won't go that easy on us. If all you had to do to survive was hide…there would have been more survivors five years ago."

Plenty of others join Mikasa in her objection.

But it's said Titans slow down at night. If you can just hold out for a little while…

"You've got a good point," Reiner says, nodding. "The question is— can we make it that long?"

(If you choose another plan, go to **139**. If you stick with this one, go to **264**.)

Things seem to have gone well for you…but you can't say the same of the other soldiers on the battlefield.

Titans are streaming into the city proper—has the vanguard already been destroyed?

As you move from building to building, you see everywhere the corpses of soldiers.

You try not to think about it, to just follow Marco's instructions…
(go to **73**)

●158

You take Mikasa's side. "Just try it!" the merchant says brashly—but Mikasa isn't one to make idle threats. She cuts him down where he stands, and he collapses to the ground.

"Pull the cart back," she orders, her expression unchanged.

One of the Garrison soldiers present says in a trembling voice, "Wh-What a tragic accident he died in. Everyone understand?"

Many around you are cowed into silence, but there is a smattering of cheers. "That's what you get, you greedy pig!" someone shouts.

"I'm going back to my station," Mikasa says calmly, and leaves.

(**Put a check mark in Flag D.** There is no associated number. Go to **83**.)

●159

You think. If you combine Eren's "Titan power" with a certain object in Trost District, it should be possible…

Look at the town map at **10**, add **104** to the number of the location you think is correct, then go to that passage. If you've chosen the right place, Commander Pixis will respond "I see."

If you don't know the answer, or if your answer is incorrect, go to **287**.

●160

You realize you might be able to aim the fixed gun directly upward and fire it.

You bring your idea to the soldiers assigned to this area.

"We should have some blank training rounds. They don't have any killing power, but they leave a trail of colored smoke. If we fired them into the air, they could serve as crude signal flares."

The commander seems intrigued by your idea.

"The gun's not built for that. The recoil might make it unusable. And even if it fired, there's no guarantee the bullet would get high enough into the air, or that the Survey Corps would notice if it did. We don't even know if they would understand what it meant if they saw it. ...But it's better than sitting here and letting the Titans have their way with us."

And with that, he gives his permission.

The cannon is fired into the air. The blank howls into the sky, trailing colored smoke. A cheer goes up from the soldiers on the wall.

(Put a check mark in **Flag L.** Along with it, remember the number **20**, or write this number on your Battle Record Sheet. Any other trainees who take up your struggle on this same battlefield after your death may also use this number. This is because the action you just took will be meaningful. Go back to **72** and choose another action.)

●161

As you watch him from behind, Levi stops, a disgusted look on his face. He seems to have gotten oil on his hands while walking through the impromptu camp. Frowning wordlessly, he reaches into his bag and pulls out a handkerchief, with which he wipes the grime away. The handkerchief is strikingly clean, and folded neatly.

It seems the legendary captain is a bit of a neat freak…much to your surprise. (Go to **162**)

●162

Apparently, the Survey Corps could tell something was wrong, and decided to come back—they even sent Captain Levi and several others ahead on horseback with lightened equipment to speed their pace.

Thankfully, this allowed them to reach you in time to help culminate the plan.

The soldiers from the Survey Corps are few in number, but their impact is great. And their presence gives the plan a much better chance of succeeding, as well.

Captain Levi and the others join the defense of the Titan, Eren.

Now, decide once more which group you would like to join.

Help Levi defend Eren (Go to **210**)

Trust Levi, and join the rear guard that's drawing off the Titans (Go to **225**)

They may be excellent soldiers, but the big picture hasn't changed. You value your life and decide to run (Go to **290**)

•163

You are at the southernmost point of Trost District, near the outer wall.

You hear occasional explosions and see dark smoke billowing up.

The cannons are firing. But they don't mean much against the Titans, with their ability to regenerate lost body parts.

You hear someone shouting distantly in between fusillades:

"The vanguard was supposed to strike the finishing blow against the Titans—but they've been wiped out. And we can't stop them with the cannons alone!"

Near the gate you can already see wrecked guns and soldiers' bodies. You…

Descend to ground level and join the cannon regiment (Go to **123**)

Engage the Titans and try to finish them off (Go to **101**)

Ascend the outer wall (Go to **280**)

•164

If Armin is alive, go to **150**.

If not…well, you of all people should know it. Go back to **232** and handle things yourself.

•165

Jean, Connie, and the others are gathered on a rooftop.

Among them, you see Armin, crouched and pale. Wasn't he a member of Squad 34? Eren's squad? A murmur runs through your gathered comrades.

"Hmph. Squad 34 is gone, except for its weakest member?" the freckled girl spits out.

"What a thing to say!" Krista exclaims, taking Armin's part.

"That's my Krista! After this mission is over, marry me!" the freckled girl says sarcastically. It's the same attitude she's always had, but sharper than usual.

Everyone on this battlefield seems to be struggling to hold onto themselves.

You offer Armin your hand, but he simply stares at it, then suddenly stands. "I'm sorry I caused problems! I'll meet up with the rear guard!"

Then he heads for the rear, alone. He seemed calm—but was he really okay?

(**Mark Eren Yeager and Squad 34 dead** and go to **195**.)

●166

This is his plan.

As things stand, the Titans that had been swarming the headquarters building are no longer a problem. The mysterious Titan outside has taken care of them all...or at least drawn them off.

Taking advantage of that respite, a large number of you will board the lift to the first floor. Since Titans are drawn to crowds of people, that should lure them toward the center of the room. Thereupon, the people on the lift will shoot them with guns prepared beforehand. Naturally, the Titans will regenerate, but the goal is only to blind them for an instant.

Another contingent hiding among the rafters will simultaneously leap down and attack the Titans' weak points.

If everything goes well, all the Titans will die at once.

But if even one person fails—if even one Titan is left alive—then, bereft of vertical maneuvering, you will all be killed.

Everyone nods, agreeing to the plan despite the risks.

First you have to prepare the guns. In the storehouse, you find dusty rifles belonging to the Military Police Brigade. They're old weapons that

would never have been any use against a Titan, but for this plan you'll need them. You were trained in the use of firearms. You assumed it was as useless as hand-to-hand combat. Who knew this was how that training would serve you?

Everyone who can fit climbs onto the lift. They're the bait. The people with guns surround them along the edge of the lift. They will try to protect the bait from the encroaching Titans, and blind the monsters as well.

Then there is the most crucial role, those who will finish off the Titans. For this you pick the most accomplished of your companions. Mikasa and Jean, Sasha and Connie. And of course Annie, Reiner, and Bertolt.

This latter group secret themselves among the beams of the ceiling, ready to leap on the Titans the moment the guns fire. Without their vertical maneuvering equipment, they'll only have one chance, as they jump.

All is ready. You get in position as well.

Now... How many Titans are on the first floor that you have to kill?

Go to the passage which equals that number added to the number of your training class (i.e., you are the ___th Training Corps). For example, if you were the 87th Training Corps and there were 13 Titans to kill, you would go to 100. If you choose the right answer, you will see the words "The plan...succeeded."

If you don't know the answer, or if you answer incorrectly, go to **250**.

•167

(Increase your **Affinity with Armin** by 1.)

Armin explains his plan…

(Check your Battle Record Sheet. **If Eren is dead**, go to **166**. **If he is alive**, go to **173**.)

•168

You entrust Krista with the command, but deep inside, you hope she'll get hurt.

That's right. You've never liked this goody two-shoes, not since training.

The freckled girl is right. She's soft.

You catch the freckled girl's eye, but she only frowns and glares at you.

(If you go ahead with this course of action, go to **185**. If you're having second thoughts, go to **79** and choose again.)

•169

"I don't need you to tell me that," Mikasa says with a frosty look. "Eren already said the same thing."

Mikasa seems to have regained her composure. (Go to **84**)

•170

The other side of the wall is overflowing with evacuated soldiers and citizens.

Voices everywhere try to confirm the safety of family, friends, comrades.

You look for other trainees from your class. You see Krista and the freckled girl who is forever at her side, and head toward them.

"Thank goodness you're all right!"

A smile spreads over Krista's face; she seems genuinely thrilled to see you.

(Increase your **Affinity with Krista** by 1 and go to 178.)

●**171**

A member of another squad brings terrible news. The city's headquarters building has been mobbed by Titans, and you can no longer resupply your vertical maneuvering equipment with fresh gas.

In order for such a small machine to propel a person at such high speed, the vertical maneuvering equipment uses pressurized gas, and uses it at a tremendous rate. A battle as long as this one would normally require several resupplies. You had been confident that you would be able to get a fresh supply from headquarters. To think that the building has been overwhelmed...

Even if you conserve your gas, you don't know how much longer it will last... (Go to 124)

You all use vertical maneuvering to position yourselves on the rooftops.

There, you join the middle guard, protecting the center of Trost District.

You look to the south, where the vanguard stands. Between the buildings you can see the vast silhouettes of Titans. And they're coming closer. Maybe the vanguard alone couldn't fend off the Titans' onslaught.

All of you will soon have to fight.

Now… Who do you choose as your leader?

Jean: "Huh? You want me to take command?"

Marco: "It's a heavy responsibility, but I'll do my best."

Sasha: "I'm so hungry…"

Krista: "We have to help our comrades. But I don't want to put everyone at risk!"

Jean (Go to **140**)

Marco (Go to **66**)

Sasha (Go to **256**)

Krista (Go to **102**)

This is the plan.

You'll take advantage of the Titans' tendency to be attracted to large groups of people by using a group of your comrades as bait. A smaller group will then use that opening to grab the gas tanks. If even one of you can get gas, you could fight using vertical maneuvering. While that person is resisting, more might get gas and join the fight. Once all of you are resupplied, you can get out of here…

Your companions listen to your idea with pale, downcast faces.

The chance of success is not high, and whether it works or not, some people are bound to be sacrificed.

You have no idea how many may die executing this plan…and you don't expect many volunteers to be the bait.

"Let's draw straws to decide who does what," somebody says.

"No," someone else says. "We need every edge we can get. We have to put our best people on reclaiming the canisters."

It's only logical—but a dark cloud has settled over your companions.

(Check your Battle Record Sheet. **If Eren is alive**, go to **125**. **If not**, go to **82**.)

●174

A shockwave runs through the area, rocking everything around you.

For a moment, you're not sure what happened.

A second Titan, as big as the first, appears—and then slams its giant fist into the Titan that attacked Mikasa, sending it flying.

The shockwave was the product of 15-meter Titans, the size of three-story buildings, having a fist fight.

The Titan who got hit falls to the ground with a resounding crash, trailing bits of flesh. The Titan who hit it gives an animal bellow, and continues to maul its fallen foe.

It doesn't even look at you or Mikasa.

A Titan that ignores humans? That fights other Titans? You've never heard of such a thing.

The scenery quakes, the air rattles.

And you can't believe what you're seeing with your own eyes.

Mikasa is looking up at the Titan, her eyes wide… (Go to **239**)

●175

For a moment, you can't tell what's happened.

A 15-meter Titan is there. On top of the half-ruined building. (Go to **260**)

•176

You whisper the details of your plan into Mikasa's ear.

You will distract the commander assigned to the two of you, giving her a chance to run for the vanguard.

Mikasa hesitates, but you insist:

"A soldier like you can do the most good on the front line. If you can stop the Titans up there, this area will be safe."

Your words seem to convince her. She gives you a word of thanks, and turns toward the front.

You have a feeling you've done a good thing. (Increase your **Affinity with Mikasa** by 1 and go to **105**.)

•177

You talk and talk, trying to comfort Mikasa.

But all your words seem to drift into the empty air.

Armin is broken, weeping.

Mikasa, who seems fearsomely alert, says to him, "This is no time to be getting sentimental." Then she turns to you and adds, "So…you can stop."

(Increase your **Affinity with Mikasa** by 1 and go to **117**.)

●178

You and the others retreat to the safe zone beyond the inner wall.

Krista and her friend the freckled girl are with you, but you don't see any other members of the 104th Training Corps.

The battle with the Titans did tremendous damage; the Garrison is in an uproar. The one consolation is that all of the citizens were able to evacuate safely...

You receive news of your friends' deaths in battle. Franz and Hannah's names are among them. In your mind's eye, you picture the happy couple...

(Mark **Franz Kefka** and **Hannah Diamant dead**, and go to **237**.)

●179

You are completely focused on killing the Titan. You sink your blades into its massive shoulders.

It's not enough. The Titan turns toward you. On its face is a thin smile.

A giant hand reaches out for you. In midair, you are unable to dodge it, and it grabs you...

(Increase your **Affinity with Mikasa** by **1**, and go to **174**.)

●180

The Titan who swallowed Thomas turns as if nothing had happened and heads off in a new direction, smashing buildings as it goes.

"Wait, damn you!" Eren says in a frenzy, and without a moment's thought he follows it with vertical maneuvering.

No! you think, and at that moment a giant face appears beneath Eren, and bites at him.

It's a Titan that had been hidden in the shadows of the building. Seven meters. The chasm of its mouth extends from ear to ear across its huge face.

It tears off Eren's leg. He loses his balance; his body tumbles through the air, slamming into the roof of the next building. (Go to 121)

●181

You try to drag the wailing Hannah away.

If only you and a wounded comrade are present with Hannah, you will have to abandon your wounded friend. (You are unable to carry both Hannah and the other person by yourself.)

If this is not the case...mark only Franz Kefka dead and go to 142

If this is the case, and you leave your wounded friend to rescue Hannah...mark Franz Kefka and the wounded comrade dead, and go to 142

If you decide to abandon Hannah after all...go to 221

You look around, hoping to help the wounded. You have to get to whoever you can before the Titans show up... But all you can see are corpses. The soldiers who manned the cannons a moment ago now lie motionless beside the ruins of their guns.

You call out at the top of your voice, but there's no answer.

Nearby, you spot a soldier half buried under rubble.

You desperately pull the debris away. You take his arm and tug.

...He seems oddly light.

That's when you realize everything below his waist is gone, crushed into a bloody soup.

Terror grips you.

Just run (Go to **136**)

Ascend the wall (Go to **65**)

•183

You received the order to advance because the vanguard has already been destroyed.

The Titans are pouring in. The forward part of the middle guard tried to stop them, but they didn't last long. Now soldiers all over town are engaged in desperate battles with the Titans wandering the streets.

"Damn it all," Jean says archly.

As your friends and the more experienced soldiers drop one after another, you continue the struggle as the Titans press in.

You wonder how much time has passed... (Go to **87**)

•184

With the gas left in your vertical maneuvering equipment, you and Mikasa are able to make it to the headquarters building. You owe this to the mysterious Titan, which fought off other Titans along the way as if to help you.

You recognize several of the faces inside. Jean, Connie, Sasha, Marco...everyone seems to have made it here safely.

"Glad you made it."

"Yeah, but...what's that?"

"A Titan...fighting Titans?"

Your friends' attention is focused on the scene outside the window.

"A Titan that prefers to attack Titans...I believe it's an Abnormal," Mikasa says. "It's thanks to him that we made it here."

The two of you look at each other and nod. You'll keep to yourself the fact that you think the Titan is Eren. After all, even you can still hardly believe it.

Some of your comrades ask whether Eren is alive, but you only shake your head silently in answer.

(**Mark Eren Yeager dead. Whether this truly signifies death, you will find out eventually.**)

"We might be able to use that Titan to get into Headquarters and get some gas," you tell everyone.

"Are you sure you understand that Titan?" Reiner says with an uncharacteristic note of panic.

You tell him that no, honestly, you don't.

It's a very high-stakes gamble…

"Fine, let's gamble," Jean says. "Sounds good to me. There's seven three- and four-meter Titans on the first floor, where the gas is. We were just talking about whether we should all just run in there together—even though it'd probably get us killed."

As you listen, you start to form a plan…

(Increase your **Affinity with Eren** and your **Affinity with Mikasa** by 1 each, then go to **166**.)

•185

In the ensuing battle, just as you expected, one after another of your comrades are slain by the Titans.

It's the fault of your soft-headed commander, Krista.

Each time someone dies she weeps afresh, but you can see them for the crocodile tears they are. Protect your other friends and keep everyone out of danger? As if it were ever that easy.

At times, she faces a Titan to help one of your comrades, without regard for her own safety.

You have no intention of letting that happen. Now that she's doomed the lot of you, she can't sacrifice herself just to make herself feel better.

You plan to attack her when you're alone, just the two of you, hidden somewhere.

That freckled girl is a problem. She's forever by Krista's side. But you wait for your moment, a moment when the freckled girl isn't there, and then you draw near to Krista. (Go to **202**)

•186

There's good news. Members of the 104th Training Corps have returned safely.

You're told they risked everything to retake Headquarters and were able to resupply themselves with gas.

But your surviving comrades, it seems, are very few, and exhaustion is written all too clearly on their faces.

You can't blame them—they've been through hell.

"There's more to it than that," one of them, Jean, mutters, his face white. "Eren... A Titan... No. We've been ordered not to talk about it. But...a story this big, no way it'll stay quiet for long." (Go to **110**)

●**187**

You do your duty where you are.

A single soldier should not be moved by the fortunes of the battle-field.

You'll do what you were told to do, where you were told to do it...

Humankind's terrible fight will continue, long into the future...

(Not-Good Ending / A Soldier's Duty)

●**188**

A short time later...

You are now atop the wall, looking down on Trost.

The city has been overrun by Titans. You see the shapes of them wandering among the buildings.

Above it all hangs an incongruously blue sky.

On top of the wall. Nearby, Eren is talking with a bald man. Commander Dot Pixis. In charge of the defense of the entire southern region, and famous lifelong perv.

The commander himself appeared on the battlefield at the head of a regiment of reinforcements. He must have responded the moment a runner came to inform him of the Titan attack. Without his prompt action, it might have taken days longer for reinforcements to arrive.

Commander Pixis intervened with the local guard captain at the last possible second and stopped him from attacking Eren.

That meant he'd saved you, as well.

"Earlier, you said—you think that with your 'Titan Power' or whatever it is, it would be possible to retake Trost District," Commander Pixis says. "Do you really believe that? Perhaps you could tell me what you had in mind."

You…

Leave it to Armin (Go to **223**)

Answer yourself (if Armin is not here, you must answer yourself) (Go to **159**)

•189

This was Commander Pixis' plan.

First, the majority of the soldiers, including his reinforcements, would gather on top of the wall. This was step one: to use the Titans' attraction to the largest nearby group of humans to get them all in one place.

Once that had been achieved, Eren in Titan form would pick up the boulder and use it to block the hole. A small number of elite members of the Garrison and other picked soldiers would act as his support.

Naturally, it would be impossible to draw off every Titan, and there was no accounting for Abnormals, so the support group would be in sig-

COMMANDER PIXIS...!

nificant danger.

The group distracting the Titans would hardly be safe, either. It might be better than direct engagement, but some measure of losses was to be expected. In addition, some combat action might be required to keep the Titans at bay. If the Survey Corps with its wealth of experience were available, there might be another way, but this was the best thing he could think of under the circumstances.

Now…which role do you take?

Protect the Titan Eren (Go to **134**)

Rear support distracting the Titans (Go to **225**)

It doesn't sound like leaving will be held against you—run (Go to **290**)

If you know the number associated with Flag L, you may go to 189 + that number

●**190**

"I just don't want to die like a dog, that's all," Rico says, almost shouting.

Perhaps it's her dudgeon that causes her to look at even you, who agreed with her, with hard eyes.

She's probably no happier about this outcome than the rest of you. (Go to **269**)

●**191**

You are fighting in the streets of Trost alongside other members of the

104th Training Corps.

Jean: "Try to coordinate with the others as much as possible. Attack the Titans if you think you've got a real opportunity—but do it carefully."

Reiner: "The goal is to slow down as many Titans as we can. Let's split up. They won't target a small unit."

Sasha: "I'm so hungry!"

Such are the words of your friends. Now, you...

Try to coordinate with the others as much as possible (Go to **228**)

Split up to take on the largest number of Titans (Go to **207**)

Are also very hungry (Go to **255**)

●192

The Garrison soldier raises his eyebrows at your words.

"How dare a mere trainee—!" He moves to hit you.

"Stand down." A woman with glasses and an air of command stops him. "Are we scared? You're welcome to see it that way. We don't want to die in vain, nor do we want to send others to do so."

Whatever the case, you seem to have made the wrong move.

You ask several more times after that, but your pleas fall on deaf ears. (Go to 144)

●193

"Trainee Eren. Can you block the hole?"

This time, Commander Pixis directs the question at Eren. "Can you block the hole in the gate with your Titan power?"

You are confident what his answer will be. He responds with conviction, ready to gamble on his friend's plan.

"I can, and I will. No matter what!" (Go to 197)

●194

"I'll...kill them..." Eren mutters in his sleep. You hate to imagine what dreams he is having.

Then, suddenly, he opens his eyes.

"Hey. Is everyone all right? How's the battle going? What about the Titans?"

In those words, you hear the Eren you know.

But… The words he spoke in his sleep couldn't have been worse.

"Hey, he said he'll kill us!"

"I knew he planned to slaughter us humans…"

The voices are those of the soldiers just nearby.

The ones surrounding you with their weapons at the ready. (Go to 208)

•195

You part ways with Jean and the others again, and resume your search and rescue activities.

Corpses are piling up all around the battlefield. You find the bodies of two fellow trainees… It's Franz and Hannah. Their bodies are close, almost cradling each other. They must have been together until the end.

Once more, you wonder how much time has passed…

At last, you hear the retreat bell sound. That means the populace has finished its evacuation.

"All that, and we weren't able to save anybody," Krista says in a voice heavy with grief.

The surviving soldiers are withdrawing with evident relief.

The two of you join them, passing beyond the wall and into safety.

(Mark Franz Kefka and Hannah Diamant dead and go to **91.)**

•196☆

Several Titans are already headed for your position.

The plan had been to seal the hole quickly, before any Titans arrived—but that plan is in ruins.

"The plan has failed," says Rico, a member of the guard unit, with profound regret. "There's nothing we can do. We won't be able to extract him under the circumstances, either. Let's leave Eren here and exfil."

Mikasa opposes this vigorously. She draws her blade; she appears ready to fight anyone who would abandon Eren.

Then Ian, the commander of the guard unit, says:

"We'll deal with those encroaching Titans. We can't leave Eren here. We've got to bring him to his senses, or get him out of that Titan body, somehow. We've got to buy him some time."

Rico and Mitabi object, naturally. There's no guarantee Eren will come to his senses, or that he won't go berserk again if he does.

You…

Take Rico's side (Go to **190**)

Take Mikasa's side (Go to **230**)

Take Ian's side (Go to **241**)

●197

From atop the wall, Commander Pixis addresses the assembled soldiers. He has a booming voice that all the soldiers can hear clearly, even though he is 50 meters above them.

He tells them about the plan, which is to use Eren's Titan form's strength to plug the hole in the outer wall. And he tells them that the support of every soldier will be needed for this operation.

A murmur of unease runs through the ranks.

Can that hole be filled? It seems impossible. And the idea of a human who can transform into a Titan beggars the imagination.

And for the sake of this unbelievable plan, they are to enter a city swarming with Titans, risk their lives?

More than anyone else, the fear grips those who have had their first experience of real combat this day.

"You expect me to give up my life for some nonsense like that?! What do you take us for?! We're...We're not disposable blades!" sobs Daz, another trainee.

Several soldiers break from the ranks and begin to run.

"If we're all just going to die," someone says, "I want to spend my last moments with my family!"

"Desertion in the face of the enemy is a capital offense!" bellows the guard captain, drawing his sword and standing in front of the fleeing soldiers. But they don't stop.

Order seems to be collapsing. It looks like nothing can be done.

"Upon my order!" Commander Pixis's voice rings out again. "Anyone who leaves right now will go unpunished!"

The unexpected words stop even the would-be deserters in their tracks.

"If you have given in to your fear of the Titans, you will never be able to stand against them! Anyone who has succumbed to terror of the Titans should leave here! And..." His voice hangs in the air. "...all those who wish for their friends, their families, their loved ones to feel that same fear, they too should go!"

The square stands silent as the soldiers absorb the commander's words.

Those who once sought to run now get back in line. Some seem resigned. Others struggle to control themselves.

The commander's words were not intended to intimidate or to cajole, or to manipulate anyone. They are simply the truth. If the Titans are not stopped here, if this wall does not stand, there will be nothing to stop the Titans from feasting on the rest of humanity.

Commander Pixis addresses the assembled crowd once more. "We cannot die inside yet another wall! Given the choice, die here!"

It is not an order or a command. It is a leader's heartfelt request of you soldiers. (Go to **189**)

You work together with Krista. The streets of Trost are swarming with Titans, and they have killed more soldiers than you can count.

From afar, people clustered around the Titans look like tiny bugs. Even now, the scene seems somehow unreal.

In fact, at this moment, you can see human forms and two Titans far away.

One of the Titans is lanky and long-haired, and wears a look of grief. The other is rotund and bald, with a neat beard around its mouth. From this distance, they almost look comical, and that makes them all the more unsettling.

The two of them sweep away the little bugs surrounding them.

You know that in reality, those bugs are people fighting desperately, trying to stay alive.

You…

Know they are beyond help. Leave them to their fate (Go to **75**)

Go to rescue them after the Titans have left (Go to **113**)

(You may also go to **100** at this point. Mark this page so you can come back to it afterward.)

(For choosing this action, increase your Affinity with Mikasa by 1)

Mikasa leaps through the city with incredible agility.

She strikes down every Titan in her path, slicing into the backs of their necks without slowing down.

Some of your friends admire her; this is just what they expect from Mikasa. But all you can think is how reckless her actions look.

Eren's death must have affected her deeply…

Suddenly, Mikasa's body freezes in midair.

She's out of gas.

Normally, she would never have let herself run out of gas. You knew she wasn't thinking straight.

Without the ability to send out or roll up her guide wires, movement is impossible. Mikasa slams into the side of a building.

She bounces off the wall onto the ground. Thankfully, the awning of a street stall catches her, and she isn't critically injured.

But she is lying on the pavement, motionless.

And you see a Titan coming.

You…

Attack the Titan to help Mikasa (Go to **179**)

Call out in a loud voice (Go to **235**)

A lot happens after the battle.

The members of the 104th Training Corps go their separate ways. The next time you all see each other is for Franz and Hannah's wedding.

You're invited, too, and it's a chance to see familiar faces.

Franz is in formal clothes, Hannah's wearing a wedding dress. They look as sweet as ever. You all cheer, but so far from looking embarrassed, they just seem more comfortable together than ever.

You're thrilled to see all your classmates again. Eren and Jean manage to fight despite the celebratory mood, and Sasha is more interested in the buffet than the bride. No one has changed a bit. ...No, maybe they have, but together you're transported back to that time.

Finally the ceremony begins. Hannah is radiant with joy in her simple white dress. Mikasa and Krista both study her closely. They must be picturing what they would look like in a dress like that.

The jubilant bride and groom hold fast to each other amidst the approving shouts of their friends.

This world is still harsh, still cruel. But surely you can afford yourselves a moment's joy like this.

Hannah throws the bouquet into the air. The other girls reach out, each hoping to be the next bride. You don't see who catches it.

(The End / An Ordinary Moment of Happiness)

●201

"You're asking me?"

Levi glares at you.

"If I had my way, I would beat the pulp out of someone so useless."

Then he puts his face up close to yours and goes on:

"But I don't know anything about your precious Eren. Isn't that your business? We in the Survey Corps have been in actual combat, and I have never seen anything as ridiculous as a person who could turn into a Titan. But I suppose my experience doesn't serve me in this case. I guess I'll have to rely on you, even if you know barely more about it than I do. Can we trust him? Can we use him? ...I'll leave it to your judgment."

With that, Levi makes to leap in the direction of the Titans.

"I was assigned to protect your little friend. My people and I will not let some mere Titan get close to you."

(Go to 269)

●202

You are caught by a Titan that appeared from nowhere.

You didn't sense anything nearby a moment ago—! An Abnormal?

The Titan seems somehow feminine. It looks at you with eyes that convey emotion.

If nothing else...it looks like Krista was able to escape.

How ironic, that you should give your life to save her.

The Titan squeezes. (Go to 14)

You withdraw.

You had no choice. What could you, a lone trainee, have done…?

From behind you come the voices of the elite soldiers, doomed to die, and the moaning of the Titans that tear at Eren's motionless body.

"I see," Commander Pixis says gratefully as you speak. "Thank you for your report. As the one who led the operation, I accept full responsibility."

The plan claimed the lives of a vast number of soldiers, and it ended in failure.

Behind you, Wall Rose is dyed the color of blood by the setting sun. How long will humanity be able to hold this wall…?

(Not Good Ending / Failure of the Reclamation Plan)

You and the others head into town to rescue your surviving comrades.

More and more Titans flood the city streets.

The rescue party takes more than a few casualties itself…but you are able to save many of your friends.

Other members of your training regiment thank you profusely when you bring them gas tanks.

"You saved our necks," says one of the people you help—Jean. "We were about to storm the headquarters building when you guys showed up. Might've cost us our lives."

You see Mikasa among those who made it out safely. Nothing less from your top graduate.

You look a little closer. Mikasa is holding a boy.

It's Eren. You can't believe your own eyes. Eren was supposed to be dead… His vest and vertical maneuvering equipment are gone; he's wearing only his soldier's undershirt. He's unconscious—almost as if asleep—but alive. And his arms and legs are in perfect shape. No injuries anywhere.

Some of your friends are talking nearby.

"I still can't believe it. That Titan collapsed, and Eren came out of its corpse. Could it have…been Eren all along…?"

Whatever the case, you and the others withdraw beyond the inner wall, taking the unconscious Eren with you.

(**Mark Eren Yeager not dead**, and record that he turned into a Titan. Go to **233**.)

●205

Something unforeseen has happened, you're sure of it.

You grab some of the gas canisters and make for the boulder.

As you get closer, you can see a lone Titan slumped on the ground, leaning against the boulder.

It looks like Eren in Titan form—but the top half of his head is missing, as are both his hands.

You can pick out the silhouettes of soldiers on the rooftops nearby. You land near them.

"It's great that that kid can turn into a Titan and all, but then he went nuts and started attacking the people with him."

The soldiers explain the situation to you with long looks.

"He ended up smashing his own head in, and... Well, you see. He's not going to be carrying any boulder anytime soon."

It's worse than you imagined. The only upside is that the soldiers are grateful for the tanks of gas. (Go to **231**)

You apply to join the Survey Corps.

More than a few of your classmates from the 104th Training Corps do the same.

Many were surprised, though, when word went around that Jean Kirstein is among the applicants.

His attitude had always been, "Huh? No way, I'm not like Eren. I don't have a death wish. And anyway, no one's gonna convince me to risk my life for anything."

The truth is, when Commander Erwin addressed the trainees, not attempting to hide the facts—that the casualty rate among the Survey Corps had been 90% over the last five years, that half of all new recruits died on their first expedition outside the wall—many of the would-be applicants walked away.

Jean, pale and gritting his teeth, had been one of those who stayed.

"Dammit. Why should I join the...the Survey Corps..."

He seemed to mock himself even in his resolution.

You wondered what had driven him to it, but when you asked he only shouted and glared at you.

Some time later...

You are lining up the horses during an expedition outside the wall—yes, the very expedition from which half of you will not return—when he suddenly tells you.

"Someone said to me once…that I had the makings of a commander. Even though honestly, I think he was the one who should've been in charge."

Then he looks at you like a thug with a nasty idea. Maybe he thinks he's smiling. You think maybe sometimes that face has worked against this man, Jean.

"You know why he said that? It's because I'm weak. What a laugh, huh?"

Somehow, you think you have a sense of what Jean's mysterious mentor was trying to say.

Jean is weak, but that means he understands what it is to be weak. As you, as many people, are. Not heroes. Just regular people.

You think maybe you could follow this uncertain youth.

But be that as it may, first the two of you must survive.

You take your horse's reins in your hand, and join the rest of the Survey Corps.

(The End / Jean Kirstein of the Survey Corps)

●207

You put some distance between yourself and your friends, and then you act.

You're confident you can distract the Titans. But to actually kill one, alone, is difficult.

You see Annie and Reiner, two of the top students in your trainee class, acting on their own. Maybe that's best for the truly skilled.

Regardless, you forge ahead.

You don't have to worry about killing them. You just have to get their attention; slowing them down is the real goal. (Go to **294**)

●208

It doesn't look like things can get much worse. You were past the wall, supposed to finally be safe, and now you're surrounded by your fellow soldiers.

Members of the Garrison are lined up shoulder to shoulder, blades drawn. They watch you, ready to fight at any moment. The fixed guns are aimed at you from atop the wall. Those are supposed to be used against Titans.

All this out of a surfeit of fear about Eren.

No matter what you and your friends say, terror deafens the guard captain and his soldiers. But if you hadn't tried to talk to them, Eren might have been "dealt with" before he even woke up.

"Trainee Yeager!" the guard captain shouts.

The fact that the captain, responsible for all the soldiers in Trost District, immediately came out to deal with things personally shows just how dire he thinks the situation is.

His voice is shaking; his words seem to catch in his throat.

"I'll ask you plainly. What are you? A man? Or a Titan?"

"I... I don't understand the question!" Eren answers. His voice is shaking, too.

How could he? Even you don't understand what's happening.

It's true Eren became a Titan. But is he, ultimately, a human like you—albeit one with the power to transform into a Titan—or is he now a Titan in human form?

You...

Trust Eren! (Go to **273**)

Do not trust Eren (Go to **229**)

A commotion breaks out in the camp as the soldiers are preparing.

Word is that a Survey Corps squad has returned.

With the gate in its current state, they climbed the wall to get back into the city.

Several people come walking by wearing military uniforms, as well as capes designed for activities outside the wall.

They carry themselves differently from the Garrison. With your newly-gained combat experience, you can tell. These are people who have survived not one fight, but many, against the Titans.

They're coming toward you at a brisk pace.

The man who appears to be their leader calls out to you:

"You. Where's the commander of the guard unit?"

The man is short, but his gaze is sharp, and he never seems to make an unnecessary movement. His very existence is somehow inspiring.

You tell him where to find the command unit, and he spins on his heel and departs with his soldiers. You see the "Wings of Freedom" crest on his back—the symbol of the Survey Corps.

A whisper runs through the camp: "That's Captain Levi!" Many sound deeply impressed.

It wasn't possible to communicate with the Survey Corps once they left on their expedition; no one even knew where exactly they were. But they seem to have sensed that Trost was in trouble, and come back.

Captain Levi is exceptional even among the elite troops of the Survey Corps. He's known as "humanity's strongest soldier" and is said to be as strong as an entire brigade. You know rumor tends to exaggerate, but he sounds impressive nonetheless. (Go to **161**)

● **210**

You work with Captain Levi and several other Survey Corps soldiers.

In the future, when you see a star (☆) after a number, you may add 5 to it and go to that section. This represents the help you get from Levi and his troops.

(Commit this to memory or make a note of it, then return to protecting Eren. Go to **134**.)

●211

"…What?" Mikasa's eyes widen at your words. "No…I can't do that."

What do you say?

"You can do the most good in the front. Stop the Titans there and we'll be safe back here, too." (Go to 176)

Encourage Mikasa. "Eren will be fine. But if you're worried—then go to him." (Go to 103)

●212

It looks like the plan has gone awry. You don't yet know what's happened.

Has the plan failed completely? Or is there still a chance it could work?

If there is, then you have to keep the Titans from reaching Eren and the others. That's all you can do now.

You ask the commander at your position for permission to descend into the city and fight the Titans.

"Granted. Be careful, trainee."

Some of your friends have the same idea. To your surprise, Jean is among them.

You set your anchors in the wall in an explosion of guidewires, and head to the streets. (Increase your **Affinity with Jean** by 1 and go to 191.)

A reinforcement unit soon arrives.

At their head is Commander Dot Pixis, the man responsible for the whole southern territory, including Trost District. He received word of the Titan attack and acted immediately.

Not long after, the elite men and women of the Survey Corps, who had been out on an expedition, return as well, and join the guard unit.

This is how the end begins in the battle to defend Wall Rose.

Many soldiers lost their lives, but the citizens were able to safely evacuate, and you were able to shore up the defenses.

Compared to the tragedy in Shiganshina District five years ago, there is little to complain about today.

Wall Rose is safe, but Trost has become a city infested by Titans.

Everyone is constantly on high alert, because you don't know when the inner wall may be broken down.

It's humanity's front line, the most dangerous place in the world, but also a prime spot for the Survey Corps to risk a little danger in order to observe the Titans and even collect samples.

You, along with Eren and the others, apply to join the Survey Corps. Your survival in this battle has earned you some credit. Now, today, you prepare to enter Trost District once more on another dangerous mission...

(Better Ending / A Narrow Victory)

Just before you must decide which unit to join…

As the trainees all mull over the question together, you have a chance to talk to Annie Leonhart.

"I don't know. You should do what you want," she says diffidently.

For her part, she's set on the Military Police Brigade: elite soldiers in the safety of the interior. It's her right as one of the top scorers in the class. If it's what she wants, she'll probably get it.

"I just want to save myself," she says, her expression never changing.

You think back to what you saw after the Battle of Trost: Annie apologizing endlessly to the corpse of her friend.

Despite what she says, you think there's more than self-interest behind Annie's decision.

She's strong-willed; you're sure she has a goal in mind.

You're determined to choose your own path, like her. As long as the choice is in your power to make, you will. (Go to **306**)

You graduate from trainees to full soldiers, each of you going off to your different regiments.

You claim your modest personal effects from the training camp and get ready to leave.

Eren comes up to you as you're packing.

"This is a memento of Armin. I want you to have it."

It's a single notebook, the pages packed with careful letters. It's his notes on tactics and strategy from your lectures during training…along with his personal observations. It's a testament to his intelligence and effort. If Armin had survived, you're sure he would have been invaluable to his unit, to humanity.

He's also written about the "outside world," information that nearly makes this notebook a forbidden object. A vast body of salt water called the "sea," water made of fire, sandy snow fields… They sound like something out of a dream, but as you read them with Armin's observations, you can't help wondering if they might really exist.

Holding the notebook, you reflect once more. You may never be like Armin. But you'll never forget the fact that he lived—a boy with an insatiable curiosity about the world outside the walls.

Maybe one day, you'll be able to experience the world he so longed to see.

(The End / Armin Arlert's Dream)

"That's right. A rescue operation would cost eight additional lives."

Behind her glasses, the female soldier's eyes are as hard as ever, but you seem to have impressed her.

"Of course reality isn't as simple as our calculations. But it's highly likely that a rescue operation now would create more casualties than it would prevent. This battle has already claimed a huge number of lives, headquarters has been overrun, and we can't count on fresh supplies. We have to put our remaining forces to best use in light of those facts.

"We'd already considered the possibility of a rescue long before you trainees brought it up."

She starts walking, and nods for you to follow.

"If you still think there's a case to be made, tell it to the captain."

You approach the guard captain just as a veteran Garrison soldier is speaking to him.

"Trainee Mikasa's a unique asset, sir. A rescue operation would be worthwhile even if she were the only one it helped! We need her for this plan—we need her to shore up the defense of the wall!"

The guard captain doesn't exactly look comprehending, but he seems moved by the soldier's words. Looks like your timing is perfect.

The bespectacled woman adds her own urging, and the guard captain nods slowly.

A rescue operation it is.

(Increase your **Affinity with Krista** by 1 and go to **126**.)

●**217**

At that moment, you suddenly spot a tall Titan.

"An Abnormal!"

It dashes straight through the building you had hoped to land on.

"Split up!"

You frantically change direction in midair. For an instant, you see the sickening details of the Titan's form.

It is thin, its body all muscles. Its arms are preternaturally long. It has a square chin, and its eyes are somehow empty. (Go to **265**)

●**218**

You and the other soldiers on the wall shoot and shoot until you've lost all sense of time.

The Titans can't reach the top of the wall, but by the same token you are isolated, unable to move.

What's become of your allies? How is the battle going?

As long as you have ammunition, you will keep at your work...

(Your fight ends here. Your companions are the ones who will determine ultimate victory or defeat. The End. You may start again in the shoes of another soldier. If you do, follow the instructions at 14.)

●219

Everyone moves according to Marco's instructions.

The plan is to lure the slower Titan to an open area, where Jean and three other capable people will jump on it from behind. The rest of you are to keep watch nearby for approaching Titans.

Incredibly, the plan works and the Titan is defeated.

You trainees have claimed your first victory in battle.

It's thanks to Marco: it was his plan, and he was the one to lure out the Titan. You realize that even in training, Marco was less concerned about his own marks than about background roles like this.

…At the same time, however, you can tell how dangerous this was. This isn't training, and Titans are living creatures. Marco might have just barely escaped being killed. (Go to 157)

●220

You face down the Titan, using all your skill in vertical maneuvering.

But you're too late. The creature swallows Thomas as you look on.

All you can think of is attacking the Titan—but your blade cuts only air. The Titan has turned around as though it hasn't even noticed you, and sets off, demolishing buildings as it goes.

The missed swing throws you off balance, and you slam into a building, the pain knocking you unconscious.

When you regain consciousness… (go to 132)

●221

There's nothing you can do. You know this scene is being repeated endlessly, everywhere on this battlefield.

You turn and leave.

(**Mark Franz Kefka and Hannah Diamant dead** and go to **142**.)

●222

From the top of the wall at the very front lines, you return to the rear to make your report. Even as you go, your allies are keeping up a hopeless barrage from atop the wall with its ruined gate. Titans are flooding the city; you can see them wandering in the streets. You run along the wall until you reach the part nearest the interior.

The other side is packed with soldiers and evacuated citizens. (Go to **178**)

●223

"Yes, sir. I did want to save him, of course, but it's also true that I have a plan," Armin responds. "The boulder in the city…Eren will turn into a Titan and carry it for us." (Go to **193**)

The Garrison soldiers confronted with Krista's impassioned pleas seem to be only humoring her.

"I see. We'll handle it."

With that, they turn and leave. You follow them. When Krista is out of earshot, you ask, "Will you really send a rescue squad?"

"Hm," says a bespectacled woman with the air of command. Then she looks at you and says, "Say there are 20 soldiers left on the field, and if we leave them, 90 percent will die. Suppose a rescue operation could save half of them. We would need 40 soldiers for the operation, and only 60 percent of them would return alive. ...Try figuring the difference in lives with and without a rescue effort."

Once you know the answer, take the difference in lives with a rescue versus without one and add it to the number of this section, then go to the section with that number. (For example, if you think ten more people would survive with a rescue effort, go to section 224 + 10. If you are correct, the bespectacled woman will say "That's right." If she doesn't, you have the wrong answer.)

If you don't know the answer, or if you gave the wrong answer, go to 122.

•225

You are assigned to be bait to distract the Titans, along with a great many other soldiers.

At no small cost—twenty percent of the soldiers die in the effort, and even this is vastly better than if you were to engage the Titans directly— you succeed in drawing the Titans to one corner of the city.

With this, the path through the city from the boulder to the gate is clear of Titans; the most crucial phase of the plan can now begin.

Eren, along with his distressingly small squadron of picked body-guards, is going to infiltrate the city. Eren will transform into a Titan and use the boulder to block the hole.

At any rate, that's what you, busy at your duty, are praying for. (Go to **108**)

•226

In any case, the plan works. You manage to exterminate the Titans inside the headquarters building, meaning you can get more gas.

You and the other survivors resupply your vertical maneuvering equipment. You'll once more be able to move freely through the air.

Talking easily now, you and your friends make for the exit. (Go to **236**)

●227

You set Eren down on the roof as quickly as you can, then use vertical maneuvering to drop to the ground.

Mikasa's fall seems to have been broken by an awning; thankfully, she's not hurt.

"Why are you here?!" She sounds at once shocked and angry.

There is a rumbling. You suddenly register that a Titan, more than ten meters tall, is directly behind you.

You rush toward Mikasa. She fights you, tries to push you away. Maybe she's telling you to save Eren, not her. …Can you have one moment today when you're not holding a struggling comrade?

Behind you, the rumbles are getting closer.

With the modicum of gas you have left, can you even carry two people? (Go to **175**)

●228

You and the others leap into action.

The hope is that together, you can bring the Titans down.

And somehow, with one after another, you succeed.

But then, too, one Titan after another seems to be converging on your position.

Is this really helping Eren and the others…? (Go to **294**)

●229

You raise both hands and run toward the guard captain and his squadron, leaving Eren to his fate.

The soldiers must believe you really are human, because they don't shoot you.

After this, the guard captain coldly gives the order to fire.

The walltop guns open up on Eren and the friends who believed in him. (Go to **240**)

●230

Mikasa seems to be on the verge of cutting down the people around her. That can only make things worse.

You tell her you know how important Eren is to her, but that she needs to calm down.

Her cheeks turn a little red.

"Important… Yes. Eren is family, after all."

It looks like you've talked her down. You start talking to the commander, Ian.

(Increase your **Affinity with Mikasa** by 1 and go to **269**.)

●231

The Titan Eren has collapsed.

So far from carrying the boulder, he tried to attack the friend who called out to him.

Steam rises from the arms and face he himself ruined, but they show no sign of regenerating. It looks like he's alive…but he doesn't move, as if he has lost consciousness. (Go to **196**)

●232

Eren, in his Titan form, has lost both hands in the top of his head; he sits motionless.

The elite squad guarding him is engaged in a desperate battle with the oncoming Titans to protect their defenseless charge.

They're excellent soldiers, but the Titans keep coming.

At this rate, they'll never be able to hold them all off.

What do you do? Observe the situation carefully before deciding.

Join the elite troops in their fight against the Titans (Go to **293**)

Rely on Armin (Go to **164**)

There's nothing to be done. Withdraw (Go to **203**)

•234

You've survived the battle in the hellish streets of Trost District, and now you withdraw.

You and several of the other trainees fall back to the rear, to safety.

At last you're in a safe place, full of Garrison soldiers. You...

Are with Eren (Go to **194**)

Are not with Eren (Go to **110**)

•235

You shout. Whether Mikasa hears you or not, you can't tell.

But she rises and takes a blade in her hand. You doubt she can best the Titan, but she isn't going to give up, either. She's a strong woman.

Even as you admire her, a Titan the size of a four-story building is coming relentlessly closer.

She sees it and takes her stance... (Go to **174**)

•236

Outside, you see numerous Titan corpses.

This is what happens when Titans fight each other. Even on a battle-field full of the enemy, this is the first time you've seen so many fallen Titans in one place...

Did that Titan take out all these others single-handedly?

At the moment, the Titan has lost both its arms, but it sinks its teeth into two other Titans, kicks them, refuses to stop fighting. It seems to have regenerative abilities like other Titans, but it looks like its powers just can't keep up…

"If we could understand what that Titan is…" somebody murmurs.

You agree…but it doesn't look like you'll have the chance.

The mysterious Titan topples the last of the nearby enemies, then sinks to its knees, exhausted. (Go to **282**)

●**237**

You ask around the guard unit in hopes of getting news about other members of the 104th Training Corps.

You learn that many of your classmates are dead, or missing in action.

(If you did not already know about the fate of Squad **34**, **mark Eren Yeager and Squad 34 dead**.)

You think of Eren and his companions, so full of spirit.

Mikasa was so close to him. What will she think when she finds out? (Go to **252**)

•238

Again and again you risk your life to protect her.

There—a Titan is about to grab Krista with its giant hand!

You leap over with vertical maneuvering. You dive between Krista and the Titan, slash the great hand with your blade. You spin around, making to attack the Titan again... (Go to **71**)

•239

Watching the Titan, you have an idea.

If you could lure it toward Headquarters, maybe it would get rid of the Titans in that area...

"All right," Mikasa nods.

You share what's left of your gas with Mikasa. It should be just enough for you to meet up with the others. (Go to **139**)

•240

Out of the smoke of gunfire and explosions a Titan towers. In its hand, humans. Eren became a Titan once more to protect those who had faith in him.

Soldiers all around cry out in terror and begin to flee.

The Titan Eren looks down at you pityingly as he rises, then sets off at a run with his friends still in his hand. No one with you is capable of stopping a 15-meter Titan. (Go to **296**)

●241

"You're taking Ian's side?" Rico says, fixing you with her intense glare.

"It isn't your fault the plan failed. Be rational," Mitabi says gently.

As for Ian...he doesn't seem any happier with your support.

Perhaps he trusts his own judgment—but knows all too well the terrible things it implies. (Go to 269)

●242

Mikasa makes for the headquarters building. It seems crazy, but then, it's better than waiting to be eaten by Titans after your gas inevitably runs out. ...No. You expect Eren will bleed out before that.

Your comrades, moved to action, also start maneuvering toward headquarters.

Some of them will probably make it.

But you, carrying a wounded friend, and Mikasa, covering both of you, have a difficult fight. Despite her exceptional maneuvering abilities, Mikasa is hard-pressed.

"Dammit! Let me fight... No. I'm useless. Just leave me here!"

Eren has set up a racket on your back. You're sure he's serious.

One Titan after another attacks you as you fly along awkwardly, but Mikasa wards them off with her incredible acrobatics.

She flies brilliantly, trailing white mist from the expelled gas.

But...

Suddenly the trail disappears. In midair, Mikasa goes stiff, is thrown sideways.

She's out of gas.

That fantastic display must have burned through what little she had left. As she falls, Mikasa points toward the headquarters building.

Leave me, she seems to say, *go*.

You…

Go to rescue Mikasa (Go to **227**)

Resolve to rescue Eren, so her sacrifice won't be in vain

(Go to **131**)

•243

Marco, having survived the brutal engagement thus far, is fighting on the same street as you are.

"Just a little longer. We have to fight…to save Eren."

He smiles at you.

It's just like you remember from training: his smile seems very warm, but his eyes are piercingly clear. Perhaps it's because of all the friends and soldiers who have died in front of them.

"If it's for a purpose, I'm not afraid to die."

He seems somehow uneasy… But now, you must fight.

Fight for victory, or at least survival. (Go to **314**)

•244

In a strained voice, you tell her the simple truth:

You are the lone survivor of Squad 34.

You feel like there must be something more to say…but no matter how you dress up the words, they won't bring your friends back.

This is the first time some of the other trainees are learning the news. You hear moans and sounds of shock.

But Mikasa herself responds with remarkable calm:

"…I see. All right."

There is no trace of grief or distress in her eyes. And to your own surprise, you find that hard to bear. (Go to **117**)

•245

You offer Armin your hand, but he simply stares at it, then suddenly stands.

"I'm sorry I caused problems! I'll meet up with the rear guard!"

Then he heads for the rear, alone. He had seemed about to collapse a moment ago—is he really okay?

Your ruminations are interrupted by Jean's voice.

"Hey. We've got orders to advance."

You have no choice. You and your comrades keep moving up. (Go to **183**)

Commander Dot Pixis, who has arrived with the reinforcements, quickly takes control of the situation.

He is the one responsible for the defense of the entire southern region, which includes Trost District, and a famous lifelong perv. That he mustered reinforcements and arrived on the field at their head so quickly speaks to his genius.

He is older, but full of life; though he has the air of command, he wears the same uniform and vertical maneuvering equipment as any other soldier.

No one knew what happened to the Titan, rumors of which were on everyone's lips, but apparently the commander had asserted his authority, and vouched for the safety of Eren and his friends.

The guard captain had been at the end of his rope, but with all the reinforcements he was able to reform his ranks.

"I heard there's a plan to strike back."

"Strike back? I know those reinforcements brought our numbers back up, but what are we going to do about those Titans?"

As unease and mistrust deepen among the soldiers, Commander Pixis informs them that he has a secret plan for a counterattack.

"The results of top-secret experiments in transforming humans into Titans."

And then he introduces...Eren.

"What's going on here?"

The soldiers around you, not least your friends, are rocked by this.

Maybe Eren did transform into a Titan—but you have a pretty good sense that this "top-secret experiments" stuff is just cover. (Go to **197**)

●**247**

You decide to fight alongside Marco.

His technique is superb, and he never hesitates to help your comrades—indeed, it seems basic to him. He distracts Titans, acts as bait.

It is one of his best virtues, but to you, it also looks dangerous.

You pause on a rooftop and bring it up with him.

Marco shrugs slightly and says, "I'm just lucky."

(In the future, when you see the words "Marco is lucky," you may add **7** to the section number and go to that section. Remember this or write it down, then go to **314**.)

•248

You approach one of the surviving horses and try to take it by the reins.

But the animal fight you, the reins flapping around. It makes a terrible whinnying, eyes wide.

This is something completely different from the calm, intelligent animals you rode during horsemanship training.

You recall that the horses used by the Survey Corps to fight Titans are of peerless lineage and receive special training; they bond with just one human for their entire lives. The horses are themselves as expensive—and as valuable—as any weapon.

Even people can hardly keep their composure under these circumstances; what more for an average horse?

You drop the reins when a giant hand grabs you. In the instant you are being crushed to death, you see the horse flee. It needn't have. Titans only attack humans, anyway. (Go to **14**)

•249

You remember Marco. He had been well-liked by everyone…

But he's gone missing in action. They didn't even find his corpse.

How many other soldiers have met the same fate in this battle? (Go to **314**)

The plan fails.

Maybe the timing of the lift was off. Maybe somebody fired at the wrong moment. Or maybe one of the Titans didn't go down...

Any number of things might have gone wrong. The chances of success always were exceptionally small.

It is no one's fault. And everyone pays the price equally. The Titans may be only three or four meters tall, but without vertical maneuvering the humans don't stand a chance. One after another of your friends are eaten by Titans.

And then they come for you...

(Bad Ending / The 104th Training Corps Annihilated at Headquarters)

The Titan Eren rises with a great roar.

Gushing steam, his ruined head and hands regenerate. And from the eyes in that the newly-formed face shines the light of the real Eren. He hefts the nearby boulder with both arms, lifts it onto his shoulders, and begins to walk.

The boulder looks heavier than he is, but he sets off for the gate. Steam rises from all over his body. For an instant, you are transfixed.

The members of the picked squad, who have survived through desperate struggle, stop and stare at him, too.

But...

Under the weight of the stone, he walks powerfully, but slowly.

At this rate the Titans in the streets will catch him, to say nothing of the ones flooding in from outside. And while he's holding that rock, he has no way to fight back... (Go to 279)

●252

You know many of your comrades have died.

And of those that remain, many are still in danger.

You learn that the city's headquarters was swarmed by Titans before anyone could withdraw, making it impossible to resupply with gas. Many of the middle guard soldiers are stranded in the city.

At this rate they will all be destroyed, unable to escape from a city of Titans. (Go to **270**)

●253

(For choosing this action, increase your Affinity with Jean by 1.)

Maneuvering gracefully, Jean leads your companions into the city.

But your gas reserves are scant, and the Titans are many.

You see several of your friends grabbed by Titans. Or their gas runs out and their vertical maneuvering equipment stops working, throwing them to the ground. Several Titans close in on them. The despairing cries of your comrades echo through the streets.

Jean has landed and is staring at one of your captured friends.

You…

Help your friends! (Go to **271**)

Defer to Jean's judgment (Go to **283**)

●254 ☆

You use vertical maneuvering, fighting as hard as you can.

You have to stop any Titans from getting through, so the elite squad's gambit won't be in vain.

You rip through the air on a trail of gas. You slice with your sword, hear the sound of the wind. Your perspective swings dizzyingly. The sky is sideways, then it's at your feet, the ground rushing to meet your head.

All over that onrushing ground, you can see soldiers, surrounded by Titans, being eaten by them.

Above the roar of the wind, screams reach your ears. You just keep slicing.

Here there are soldiers dying and despairing. And just beyond, the Titan Eren walks.

(**Mark Ian Dietrich and Mitabi Jarnach dead** and go to **302**.)

●255

You realize you are a little hungry. After all, it's not like you've had time to eat.

But hunger is a sign that you're alive. Your anxiety eases slightly.

If Sasha is alive and nearby, you think you'll tell her…

Tell her that if you both survive this battle, you should get something delicious to eat together.

And then…you return to the fight.

(Increase your **Affinity with Sasha** by 1 and go to **294**.)

•256

"F-First, let's find some food!" Sasha says. "There must be provisions that got scattered around the city in the confusion. They'll help us later…"

Everyone is predictably exasperated at this idea.

"This is no time to be joking around!" Jean yells.

"F-Food is definitely important." Krista alone tries to smooth things over.

There is some logic to what Sasha is saying, but if this battle goes south, food isn't going to save you.

(Increase your **Affinity with Sasha** by 1 and choose another leader.)

Do you make Jean your leader (go to **140**)? Or Krista (go to **102**)?

•257

You call out to Armin and head for the rear using vertical maneuvering. Armin is pale and silent, but seems to be following you.

(**Mark Eren Yeager dead**. Go to **112**.)

Suddenly, a fusillade rings out.

It's practically right next to you. What in the world happened?

Reiner jumps onto a nearby roof with his vertical maneuvering equipment without so much as asking the permission of your guards. Annie, Jean, and several others follow him.

Including you.

From the rooftop, you look toward the wall, and see an astonishing sight.

The fixed guns are turned toward the inner wall. Not toward the Titans trapped in the city; they fired at this side of the wall. The side full of your allies.

And then, through the smoke, you see what looks like a seated Titan.

Its body is incomplete, just muscles and bones.

And amidst the bones…Eren, who seems to have given birth to the thing.

(If you haven't already done so, make a note that Eren Yeager can transform into a Titan. Further, if you have marked him dead, erase the mark.)

"What…the hell…is going on?" someone asks. (Go to **246**)

At that moment, a group comes whizzing through the air.

It's Captain Levi and his elite soldiers.

Their capes flutter as they maneuver around, giving them the appearance of birds.

They make sure that the sacrifices of the soldiers who landed on the ground are made good to the full.

They assail one Titan after another. They slow down the monsters, save the soldiers on the ground, land precise blows on the Titans' weak points. They massacre the creatures.

A cheer goes up from the soldiers below.

And through the sound, Eren walks.

(Any characters marked dead in a section with a ★ by the number survive. Go to **302**.)

260

The Titan appeared so suddenly, it seemed to come from the roof of a building.

And it punched the Titan that was trying to attack Mikasa.

You've never seen two Titans fight before. The enemy Titan is thrown backward, smashing into the building.

A Titan is attacking another Titan…as if to protect a human.

The Titan looks at you. It looks like a raging monster, but its eyes have the glimmer of intelligence.

You hear Mikasa's voice:

"Eren."

You know instinctively that she's right. It makes no sense, but…that Titan is Eren. (Go to **184**)

•261

Remembering your training, you work the gun as hard as you can.

Normally it takes several people to load, aim, and fire, but you do it all by yourself—you, a trainee.

With your fumbling hands, you do it.

When you finish loading, the Titan is right in front of your eyes. You fire.

There's an explosion—a direct hit on the Titan!

Yes!

But… The creature only stumbles a bit. Part of its chest was blown away, but it soon begins to heal in a cloud of white steam. Deafened by the explosion, you can't hear what's going on around you.

A massive hand grabs you in what, to your ears, is silence. Silently it brings you to its gaping mouth.

And then, not only sound, but light vanishes. You have been eaten by a Titan. (Go to **14**)

●262

You draw your blade and plunge it into the nape of the Titan's neck.

You were watching when Eren became a Titan. If you strike here—careful not to injure the head of the real Eren inside…

You succeed. As if in response to your action, the Titan gives a great thrash.

You cling to the hilt of the blade to avoid being thrown off, and call to Eren: memories of training, his passion for killing Titans… Maybe even the dream of the world outside that you heard about from Armin.

(Increase your **Affinity with Eren** by 3 and go to **251**.)

●263

You wake up in a middle school classroom.

You must have fallen asleep. You look around the classroom: Eren and Jean are fighting again. Armin is wrapped in a blanket, and the hearts are practically streaming off Franz and Hannah.

"What do you mean, peaceful?! Those Titan kids stole my lunch again!" Eren shouts. It's true this is a pretty awful middle school—but you enjoy every day here. Everyone is happy and full of life. Don't forget, you've got Wall Beautification Club after class… **(Fin!)**

●264

You act on the plan to stay holed up in the building. More and more Titans show up nearby; you hear the disturbing sounds of them beating on the walls and ceiling, chewing on them. More than a few of your friends are grabbed by hands that come in wherever there's space.

You wonder how much time has passed... Eventually, the light outside begins to fade.

You can't see very well, and the Titans' pounding prevents you from talking. You no longer even know if anyone else is left alive.

But it will be night soon. That might be your salvation... So you struggle to go on.

And then, suddenly. With one great noise, the building shakes violently.

There's a sound like an explosion, and the headquarters, which had seemed so sturdy, begins to collapse.

You clamber out of the building in a panic.

When you look up, you see a massive Titan looming in the dusk.

Fifteen meters. It looks immensely powerful, as though its entire body were covered in armor.

Standing amidst the rubble and the bodies of your companions, all you can do is stare at it.

The last thing you see is the Armored Titan rushing at the inner wall of Trost District to break it down.

(Bad Ending / The Fall of Wall Rose)

●265

You and the others land on the roof of a nearby building.

"Is everyone okay?!"

"T-Thomas!"

You turn and see that one of your companions, Thomas, has been caught by a Titan. The lower half of his body is already in its mouth. Pale, he looks around wildly for help.

"Thomas!" Eren shouts.

You...

Rush to cut down the Titan and save Thomas (Go to **138**)

Recall your training and use vertical maneuvering to challenge the Titan (Go to **220**)

Tell Eren to calm down (Go to **153**)

(You may also go to **100** at this point. Mark this page so you can come back to it afterward.)

●266

You wonder how Eren and the others are doing outside...

As you wait, you hear rumbles and explosions.

Then your companion who has been heading things up outside returns.

"Eren... He ran out of gas and wound up in the streets..."

So that's it. Brave Eren perished for the sake of his comrades...

But then your companion's story takes an unexpected turn.

"And then... Damn. I still can't believe it. All I can do is tell you what I saw, but one minute Eren was there, and the next a Titan appeared. And for some reason, it started attacking the other Titans. It didn't even look at us humans. There's a huge Titan brawl going on outside right now..."

For an instant, thought crosses your mind: Could it be that Eren turned into a Titan and is protecting you? But you brush it away. It's not possible. Eren is dead.

(**Mark Eren Yeager dead** and go to **137**.)

•267

From that point on, Jean continues to run when a Titan approaches, fighting only when necessary.

Even when he fights, it is only so he can get away; he doesn't kill any of the Titans.

"This when our friends and the more experienced soldiers are fighting..." some of your companions say in disgust, but Jean shouts back:

"Shut up! Just distracting the Titans helps plenty. You're not gonna do any good if you're dead!" (Go to **73**)

But…

Instead of picking up the boulder, the Titan Eren begins to attack the nearby soldiers!

They take evasive maneuvers and come away unhurt, but Eren's Titan fist smashes into a building.

Eren isn't unscathed by the attack; his fist begins to gush bodily fluid. It was a bizarre act.

He seems to have forgotten about the boulder. He launches attack after attack at Mikasa as she calls to him desperately.

He shows no sign of intelligence; he's attacking humans on instinct. As if he were a normal Titan…

Perhaps he was never anything more than that.

Eren continues to flail despite his ruined fist. He takes a swing at Mikasa, who has landed near his head to try to bring him back to himself, and he ends up destroying his own face.

With a great noise, and taking half a building with him, he falls—and stops moving.

"Grr… The plan failed!"

Rico, a soldier of the Garrison and leader of the bodyguard detachment, makes a sour face and fires a signal flare.

The flare means something desperate has happened, or the plan is being aborted. It trails red smoke into the air. (Go to **231**)

Rico's eyes are hard as she thrusts a question at Ian.

"Hundreds of people have already died for your precious human weapon... and you're saying we have to bring him back so we can go through it all over again?"

"That's right... no matter how many die, we should keep trying! There's no replacement for him. Yes, the chances are abysmal. But this gamble is our only hope!" Then Ian turns the question on Rico. "Tell me... If we abandon him, how do you propose humanity beat the Titans?"

Rico has no answer.

Ian is right. Right now humanity has nothing else—not even some other "untrustworthy" weapon. If you flee now, if you survive…you will only postpone your ultimate destruction.

You, and everyone there, understand that.

Ian doesn't seem pleased to have convinced you, though.

"This is all we humans can do. Die like insects for something with no promises and no certainties. That's our fight. Our final struggle." (Go to 232)

●270

You see Krista pleading with the Garrison soldiers.

"I'm begging you. My friends are still out there. Please send someone to help them—no, send me!"

But the soldiers look at once troubled and unimpressed.

You…

Join Krista in pleading with them (Go to **92**)

Taunt them. "You afraid of a little rescue mission?" (Go to **192**)

Think it's futile to beg (Go to **224**)

●271

You fly into the crowd of Titans.

There are so many of them. Massive hands grab at you left and right. You feel your enemies taking bites out of you.

You look up to see Jean and your other comrades growing smaller in the distance.

Jean glances back, just for a second. He's far away now, but you think you see an apologetic look in his eyes.

Did your sacrifice save your friends…? (Go to **14**)

You, too, halt your vertical maneuvering and land on the ground.

The members of the picked squad smile weakly at you.

Every face is marked with terror. With drawn looks and uncertain steps, they go about getting the Titans' attention.

No one dies bravely. They all go screaming, weeping, in agony; their deaths are brutal and ugly.

But they are, undoubtedly, heroes.

You join the parade of death.

Beyond the awful cries of the perishing, Eren walks with the boulder on his shoulders.

You look up at him. To protect that hope, you, too, will walk directly toward death.

Finally, your body is grabbed by a huge hand.

And just like the others, your fear breaks you; you scream at the top of your lungs…

(**Mark either Ian Dietrich or Mitabi Jarnach dead**. One of them is saved by your actions. Go to **304**.)

•273

You trust Eren. You stand between him and the guard captain, shielding him.

Next to you, Mikasa has drawn her blade, ready to fight if she has to.

You think fast. You have to avoid a fight. Humans can't start killing each other.

You wrack your brain for ideas.

A voice pleads with the guard captain.

It says Eren himself is a way to fight the Titans, that he can give hope to humanity. That with him on our side, it might even be possible to retake Trost District.

Is that Armin's voice? Or are those words you yourself desperately shout?

Either way, the soldiers around you don't seem to want to listen.

The guard captain raises his hand mercilessly.

He's about to give the order to fire the cannons at you...

(Increase your **Affinity with Eren** and your **Affinity with Mikasa** by 1 each, then go to **188**.)

•274

After that, Krista stops doing such rash things.

You link up with Jean, Connie, and the others. It looks like they managed to survive, too. (Go to **165**)

•275

Armin, wearing a grave expression, starts talking to everyone there.

"I've got a plan. It's pretty dangerous, but if it works it could save us all. Will you hear me out?"

You…

Support Armin and listen to him (Go to **167**)

Don't listen (Go **back to 139** and think of something else)

•276

You keep on fighting the Titans with your vertical maneuvering.

There are moments when you catch sight of Armin. He is at the nape of the Titan Eren's neck and has buried a blade in it. The Titan's body gives a violent thrash in response. He's not trying to kill it. He has missed the vital point by inches. He just wants to wake Eren up. You catch glimpses of the scene. Armin shouting something at the top of his lungs. The word "Eren!" comes to you faintly on the breeze.

Your attention is taken up by the Titan in front of you.

You know Armin is fighting his own battle.

Finally… (Go to **251**)

•277

At that moment, human silhouettes fly through the air.

It's Captain Levi and the elite troops of the Survey Corps.

They slice apart Titan hands that have grabbed soldiers, Titan mouths that seek to eat them, rescuing the troops on the ground.

You're near the ruined gate. There are no buildings here. Levi and his troops use the Titans themselves as anchor points from which to maneuver.

This must be what they've learned from all that time fighting Titans outside the wall, where buildings are few. They make you think of birds, flying freely through the vast space.

The soldiers around you, who had given up all hope, let out tearful shouts of joy.

With support from the air, the chances they might be rescued improved tremendously. At the very least, no one will die in vain.

You go back to your duty.

Your duty… To draw off the enemy Titans at the risk of your own life.

(Any characters marked dead in a section with a ☆ by the number survive. Go to 312.)

•278

With so many of you pushing the cargo wagon together, it begins to move bit by bit. Or…it should have.

You wonder how much time has passed.

You fall into a reverie as you push, but are shaken from it by several large tremors.

You look toward the town, and see a horde of Titans coming your way. There are many more monsters than there are soldiers to protect you.

The warning bell rings out. Some of the soldiers on guard are shouting.

"Close the gate immediately!"

"There's nothing we can do! We have to stop the evacuation!"

The crowd panics. They scramble over the cart, trying to make it through the gate as it closes, but the road becomes clogged with shoving people. "Never mind!" the merchant shouts, "Forget the cargo!" But he is sucked into the throng of people and you lose sight of him.

And then the Titans come.

They pick people out of the crowd around the gate, popping them into their mouths one after another.

Shouts and cries rise up, mingling with the crunch of humans being chewed and eaten.

What can people do now? Maybe Wall Rose will be destroyed... But you won't see it. A Titan's hand picks you up and drops you into its gaping mouth.

(Bad Ending / Evacuation Failed)

The commander, Ian, shouts at you:

"You trainees, work with Eren. That's an order! Rico, your squad is to support them with vertical maneuvering!"

Then he turns to his own subordinates:

"Protect Eren with your lives!"

You see Mitabi's squad already on the ground. They've stopped using vertical maneuvering and are simply walking along.

They're distracting the Titans with their own bodies. When a Titan is hunting a human, it pays no attention to anything else. That will give Eren a chance to move. Such seems to be their plan.

Ian and his squad follow them.

You swallow heavily at the incredible scene.

But this is all you have left. If you had a horse, things might be different, but now all that can be given for the success of the plan is human lives.

You…

Support the troops with vertical maneuvering (Go to **254**)

Go to the ground yourself, and work with the picked squad (Go to **272**)

●280

The top of the wall, above the gate, looks almost as if it has been ground away by something. You see no sign of the fixed guns. The rail is gone, too, so there's no way to move new guns into place.

Beyond this immediate area... You hear the fixed cannons on both the inner and outer walls firing intermittently.

You make for where a few surviving guns remain atop the wall. (Go to **72**)

●281

"This ain't the time to be letting our guard down," Jean says, for some reason in an even worse mood than usual. Then he explains the situation.

He tells you how the headquarters in the city was swarmed by Titans, how you can't resupply yourselves with gas and so can't cross over the wall and get out of here. You'll be left in a city full of wandering Titans, and when your gas runs out you won't even be able to maneuver any-more—only die.

"Things could be worse, though," Armin says. "First, we survivors need to split our remaining gas between us, then we can think of a plan." (Go to **173**)

The smoking Titan corpse crumbles away.

At the nape of its neck, you think you can make out a human form.

…It's Eren.

You thought Eren was dead. What is he doing in a Titan's neck?

He has lost his jacket and his vertical maneuvering equipment; only the undershirt of his uniform remains. He's unconscious, almost as if asleep, but he's alive. What's more, his legs and arms are in perfect condition. He doesn't seem to be injured anywhere.

"Eren!" Mikasa shouts, running toward him. She catches him in her arms.

Normally calm and reserved, Mikasa sobs like a child, so loudly you can hear her from where you stand.

"What the hell's going on?"

Your companions seem every bit as confounded as you are.

For now, you need to take the sleeping Eren and get out of here…

(Mark Eren Yeager alive, then make a note that he can turn into a Titan. Go to 233.)

Jean does nothing to help your companion, but only points ahead.

"Now's our chance. This way, follow me!"

In the blink of an eye, he made the decision to leave behind those who could not be saved, in order to save those who remained.

He isn't simply running from fear. He refused to let their ultimate sacrifice go to waste.

He seizes on a gap between Titans, and slips through it in the nick of time.

A Titan's hand grabs Jean. He slips out of his boot and keeps pushing.

The two of you think only of flying, using the last of your gas.

The headquarters building is just ahead of you.

You kick in a window on the second or third floor and dive in.

As you land, you realize you're out of gas. You couldn't have cut it any closer.

Jean's spontaneous decision…seems to have been the right one.

But when you look at him, you see he doesn't have the calm, cold expression of a commander. In fact, exactly the opposite.

"How many of us made it…? Using the deaths of our comrades… How many died…on my signal?" (Go to **139**)

It's a terrible outcome… You don't even find the bodies of some of your friends.

Somebody whispers:

"To think, this was the best we could hope for. If more Titans had come in from outside, casualties would've been even worse."

Quailing, you look out the window.

A bizarre sight meets your eyes: Titans are fighting each other.

A mysterious, 15-meter Titan with black hair gives a great bellow, and slams another Titan with its fist, bites with its teeth. The other Titans must see it as an enemy, because they are swarming it.

"We don't know where he came from, but the other Titans seem drawn to him. It's thanks to him we're alive."

Now you know… Without that mysterious Titan, your losses would likely have been worse. Or perhaps the entire plan would have failed, and you would all have been annihilated.

Could that Titan be an Abnormal? Even if it is, you've never heard of a Titan like this, let alone one that arrives with such impeccable timing… (Go to **226**)

●285

Then, you spot a flying column on horseback.

The information you gave the commander seems to have helped; all the horses left in the city have been mustered.

There are only a few of them, but they've arrived at the best possible moment to ensure this precious strategy does not go to waste.

They're specially trained, top-quality horses intended for the Survey Corps. They won't take fright even in the face of the Titans. Bold animals a soldier can trust as well as his own feet.

The mounted unit moves to support the brave soldiers on the ground, using their excellent horsemanship to lead the Titans on a chase.

"Change of plans!" your commander, Ian, yells. "Link up with the mounted troops. If you've got gas left, use vertical maneuvering!"

Amidst the newly-energized soldiers, Eren lifts the great boulder onto his shoulders and begins to walk. (Go to **302**)

●286

You pull Krista back and bring her to a safe location.

"Why did you stop me? O-Our friends…"

She struggles with you; she is weeping.

Before you can say anything, the ever-present freckled girl breaks in.

"If we'd left you alone, Krista, you would've died. And if you hadn't, our friend right here would have."

At her words, Krista falls silent.

But you don't think what she says is quite true. Surely she herself would have saved Krista.

That's what you think, anyway, but the freckled girl only snorts and adds:

"Get it? Next time, think before you act." (Go to **274**)

•287

"Is that so? I had my hopes, but I guess it was too good to be true."

The commander gives a long sigh.

And with that, the battle to defend Wall Rose comes to an end.

With no way to reclaim the Titan-infested Trost District, the only thing to do now is stiffen the defenses on the far side of the inner gate.

Commander Pixis seems personally sympathetic to you and your friends, but he cannot overlook something as dangerous as a boy who can turn into a Titan. Eren is sent under guard to await a court-martial.

And no one knows how long the imperiled Wall Rose will hold…

(Not Good Ending / Failure to Reclaim Trost District)

This is how the Battle of Trost ends.

A victory for humanity—its first victory since the appearance of the Titans.

You not only survived the brutal fight, but were able to contribute to that victory.

But…the price of that triumph is staggeringly high.

A huge number of soldiers died—including many of your fellow trainees from the 104th Training Corps.

And those whose names could be added to the rolls of the dead were the lucky ones. Many more were eaten by Titans, or mangled beyond recognition. And that is to say nothing of all those who simply went missing in action.

Two days pass.

The Titans still wandering the streets of Trost District are finally dispatched by the ceaseless firing of the walltop gun emplacements and the tireless work of the Survey Corps' elite troops.

Along with the other surviving soldiers, you help the Sanitary Disposal Squad clean up the former battlefield and search for the missing. That is to say, you are tasked with discovering bodies that haven't yet been found and disposing of them. Decomposition has already begun, and you have to prevent a secondary disaster like an outbreak of disease.

You and the others gather countless bodies from throughout the city—bodies crushed, bodies maimed.

You find a disturbing mass in which several people's bodies seem to have melted together.

They are humans who were swallowed by a Titan.

Titan biology is not yet well understood, but they do not seem to have either digestive or excretory functions. Humans a Titan eats are not even absorbed into its blood or flesh, but are simply spat back up this way, like vomit. They gorge themselves on humans not for sustenance, but only to kill. The dead are left a mound of flesh, without even their dignity.

Even your friends, who survived that hellish battlefield, lose their composure at this. Some go blank in the eyes and begin muttering to themselves. Many cannot sleep in the bar-racks; many others wake screaming in the night.

As you work, you spot Annie. Annie Le-onhart, typically so calm and almost emo-tionless, stands in front of a friend's still body, murmuring.

"I'm sorry… I'm sorry…"

In the midst of all this, you run into Marco Bott.

Marco is lucky. (Go to **289**)

Marco Bott is lucky: half his face is left, so you know the body is his.

That means he can be officially listed among the deceased, rather than simply among the missing.

(**Mark Marco Bott dead.** If he was already dead, consider yourself to have found his body at this point.)

The death of the cheerful, well-liked Marco is a shock to your entire unit.

That night...

Corpses, countless corpses, are piled up and cremated. Under the circumstances, it's impossible to hold a separate funeral for everyone who died. The ashes will be buried all together...

"Why him?" Jean mutters, looking into the flames. Something about him has changed since the battle. Then, as if he's finally made up his mind, he says to all of you:

"Hey...you guys... Have you decided which branch of the military you're gonna apply to?"

His voice strained, he continues:

"I've decided. I...I'm...I'm gonna join the Survey Corps."

(You should decide which path you will take. Go to 306. If you talk with Annie, go to **214**.)

You flee the unit.

Several others run, too, including your fellow trainee, Daz. True to his word, Commander Pixis let you go.

You go back to your home, to spend a brief, peaceful time. Daz ends up coming with you. He says shamefacedly that he can't go back to his hometown.

You never hear what happened at the battle in Trost District. It's possible that humanity was victorious, but because of what happened with Eren, all information about the battle was deemed confidential...

One clear day.

With no warning whatever, you get word that Wall Rose has fallen.

There's no time to run. The rumbling footsteps of Titans are too near...

(Bad Ending / A Moment's Peace)

●291

You take the merchant's side and try to reason with Mikasa.

You tell her you'll do something about it. Above all, a soldier, sworn to protect the people, must not go around killing civilians.

Mikasa is silent for a moment... Then, with no change in her expression, she glares at you and says, "I'm going back to my station." She turns away from you and leaves.

The merchant pounds your back in elation.

"Well done! My gratitude will mean more for you than you could earn in a lifetime as a mere soldier!"

You start pushing the cart, and order the evacuees around you to help. (Go to 278)

●292

Just a moment more, and the plan will succeed.

You and the others do everything in your power to stop the Titans in the city, to draw them off, slow them down, and otherwise keep every monster you can from reaching Eren.

You keep on fighting with all your strength. So do your friends. Will you all make it through this battle in one piece? (Go to 127)

•293

You fight alongside Mikasa and the elite troops against the encroaching Titans.

You bring one down… But there are so many. And more seem to be coming every moment.

You can keep fighting, but your defeat will be only a matter of time.

(Go back to 232 and make a different choice.)

•294

A voice like a great howl sounds across the city from far off.

"Hey! Look at that," Jean calls to you from a high rooftop.

Far away, you can see a massive human shape moving. It is obscured by buildings, but you can make out its head. No… That's not its head. It's a massive round object. A boulder, moving slowly through the streets.

It's Eren.

The Titan has picked up the huge rock and is moving toward the hole in the outer gate.

You see, too, enemy Titans moving in his direction from all around the city, as if drawn to him.

"All right. Protect Eren!" Jean shouts, and then your friends take up the cry. (Go to 292)

Marco Bott is lucky: he survived the awful battle.

"But…so many of our friends didn't. It wouldn't have been surprising if I had died, too…"

Marco speaks in a strained voice as he helps with the collection of the bodies.

That night…

Corpses, countless corpses, are piled up and cremated. Under the circumstances, it's impossible to hold a separate funeral for everyone who died. Marco stares vacantly into the flames.

Jean comes up to him.

"Hey, Marco. Have you decided which branch of the military you're gonna apply to? "

When Marco answers, his eyes are strikingly clear.

"I'm still thinking about it. I always had my heart set on the Military Police Brigade…but now I'm not sure if it's right to join them."

"Haha. Well, I've decided."

Jean saw his share in this battle. The braggadocio and bravado he always used to put on are gone. So thoroughly gone, in fact, it's almost disconcerting. In a voice just the same—and completely different—from the one you know, he says:

"I've decided. I'm joining the Military Police."

(If your **Affinity with Jean** is greater than **2**, then you may also apply to the Military Police Brigade if you wish. If you do, go to **313**. Otherwise, go to **306**.)

•296

After that…

You don't know what happened to Eren and his friends.

The Corps was in no condition to chase after him, once the inner gate of Wall Rose was smashed down.

Humanity was forced to retreat to the last of its territory, behind the final barrier, Wall Sheena.

Thus…

You now reside in Ehrmich District, at the southernmost point of Wall Sheena.

You and the rest of the surviving soldiers prepare for a final, hopeless defense.

A thought flits through your mind:

What if you had trusted Eren?

(Bad Ending / Eren Flees)

●**297**

You and the surviving members of Squad 34 join the middle guard.

The Titans are relentless, but you face them down. Even the scant experience you've had in the battle so far is proving valuable.

Experienced soldiers and other members of the squad are falling in droves. And amidst it all, you're fighting for your life against a massive Titan. You wonder how much time has passed... (Go to **89**)

●**298**

You've decided it's too late to help Armin. If you can at least save Eren...

You jumped to the roof where Eren lies and take him in your arms, then begin vertical maneuvering.

You can hear Armin's screams behind you. In your arms, Eren is shouting.

"D-Damn you! We can't just leave Armin!"

You ignore him, trying to put space between the two of you and the horde of Titans. (Go to **86**)

●**299**

A short time later, you have a chance to talk with Annie Leonhart.

You try to ask her about the best unit to join, about Marco and Jean, but she's diffident.

"It's all the same to me."

You ask Annie what her plans are, and she answers with her usual unchanging expression.

"I've decided what to do. Even if it's not quite what I planned."

You think back to the fierce battle that only recently consumed Trost District. You remember the sight of Annie apologizing endlessly to the body of her fellow trainee. Maybe that's what she means by "not quite."

You sure there's something she feels she has to do, something that hasn't changed, despite everything.

Perhaps she knows that this world decrees a fate for each of us that cannot be contravened, yet she has steeled herself to stand against it just the same. She's a strong woman.

"I just want to save myself," she says, looking away from you.

And yet... You think back to what Annie said to you when you met in town.

She may really be kind. Though she spoke only a few words, you feel they changed something. Maybe the fate of the world turns on such small things.

"Hm. I wonder."

Annie smiles, just a bit sadly. And then, she leaves for the path she has to take.

(Go back to **295** and choose your own path.)

You survive the battle and decide to join the Survey Corps.

Now you are a member of the Survey Corps' special unit commanded by Captain Levi—popularly known as Squad Levi.

"Hey, don't let it go to your head, new kid." One of the senior soldiers, Oluo, glares at you intimidatingly. "I figure Captain Levi only picked you because your battle experience in Trost makes you unusual. I seriously doubt he saw any actual skill in you. Don't slow us down, now. Heh heh!"

So saying, he gives you an unsettling smile. Maybe he means it to look cool.

"Don't scare the rookies, Oluo," another of the established troops, Petra, breaks in with annoyance. She holds out her hand to you and smiles.

"You survived that awful battle, and that means you've got real experience. I'm sure the captain saw that, and that's why he picked you. Glad to have you with us."

"Right! Exactly! Your precious experience!" Hange Zoë suddenly jumps into the conversation in a booming voice. "Tell me everything about the new Titan you saw in Trost! Oooh! I wish I had been there! Now, you! You and I can talk the night through about Titans!"

Even for a member of the Survey Corps, this bespectacled woman has a great—perhaps too great—interest in Titan research. She's a strange one even in a unit full of strange ones. You've already lost count of how

many times she's made you tell her about your experiences in Trost District.

"Hey, Hange. Don't waste my subordinates' time."

It's Captain Levi. He says to you:

"There's something I want you to do."

You salute him anxiously. You would undergo any training and take on any task, no matter how difficult, if it meant remaining in the unit of the strongest man in the world.

"Good. I like that attitude." Levi hands you a broom and a rag. "Clean the headquarters again. I won't let you slack off just because you're part of my unit now."

So here you are, part of the special unit within a special unit, doing your duty to your utmost under your leader—your clean-freak leader.

(Special Ending / Captain Levi's Recruit)

It has been three days since the end of the battle in Trost District.

Mikasa is staying in lodgings near the military tribunal. Eren will be tried shortly, and those who are close to him are under house arrest and being interrogated. You suspect, though, that Mikasa would have been there whether or not she was legally confined. You know she wants to be as close to Eren as she can.

"Eren… He still hasn't opened his eyes."

He's been asleep for two days straight, and apparently still hasn't woken on this, the third day.

"What will we do if he… If he stays like this…?"

Mikasa has the anxious face of a young child. She is stroking the old scarf she always wears like a prayer. You always knew her as a woman of steel, who hardly knew how to hesitate. You've never seen her this way before.

You tell her it'll be all right. Who could leave a girl as beautiful as her waiting? And in your heart of hearts, you do believe it.

Mikasa gives you the faintest of smiles. You've never seen an expression quite like that on her face before, either.

You wonder if you might get to know her better now. Perhaps one day she'll tell you about Eren, and about that old scarf wrapped around her neck.

(The End / Mikasa's True Face)

Eren walks, a giant lumbering amongst the deaths of countless soldiers.

He's nearly to the gate.

"GOOO!" you hear someone shout—or is that your own voice?

Eren raises the great stone overhead, then flings it at the hole in the wall.

The crash of it shakes the whole city.

It is the sound of victory.

A signal flare arcs into the air. Yellow smoke: the plan has succeeded.

You, all of you, have triumphed. (Go to **303**)

●303

What happens next, you remember only as in a dream.

After the hole was blocked with the boulder, the Titan Eren, as if knowing his duty was finished, slumped to the ground and ceased to move. His body, with its extremely high temperature, steamed mightily.

As the Titans remaining in the city converged on him, you tried to save Eren by cutting his human body out of that steaming Titan form…

You were saved by soldiers who arrived on a rescue mission in the nick of time.

It was the Survey Corps, which had returned from its exploration of the outside world and climbed over the wall to get back into the city.

You were at their backs as they fought to protect you, so you had a clear view of the crest emblazoned on the Survey Corps' capes. The crest is called the "Wings of Freedom," and you will never forget it. (Go to **288**)

•304

This is how you fall, one more of this battle's innumerable nameless dead.

"The plan was a success," someone says. "Today, humanity claimed its first victory against the Titans."

"Thank God… Everyone… Everyone's death meant something."

Rico Brzenska is weeping. The elite soldier of the Garrison who once glared at you with those implacable eyes—now she cries like a little girl.

And some of those tears are for you. You wonder how many.

That's not so bad.

(The End / Nameless Hero)

"It's all thanks to you!"

The next time you see Eren Yeager, he sticks out his hand to you.

The aftermath of the battle was almost as eventful as the battle itself. So many things have happened around you and to you. Eren must not be the hot-blooded, single-minded boy he was in training any longer.

But he is still Eren.

"I wanted to thank you again, too," says Armin hesitantly, standing next to Eren. "Because of what you did…I'm alive now and can be with Eren. Thanks to you."

Then he smiles. He and Eren have been friends for a long time. You think you and he could be friends for a long time to come.

Another of Eren's old friends is there—Mikasa. But she only looks at you silently, with cold eyes. You'd like to be friends with her, too, but…

"Now," Eren says to you forcefully, "join us in stopping the Titans. And in exploring the world outside the wall!"

What he's saying seems impossible; an extravagant dream. But when he says it, you think it might just come true.

You take Eren's outstretched hand with all the strength you can muster.

(The End/Eren Yeager's Hand)

•306

You've survived the battle. But what does your future hold?

First, starting at 1, see which of the following applies to you.

1. If you have checked "Flag D," you must go to 311.

2. If you have checked "Flag L," and you fought with Captain Levi you may go to 300, or move on to 3 below.

3. If you have not checked either flag, go to 307.

•307

If any of the following apply to you, follow the instructions provided. If more than one applies, choose the person with whom you have the highest Affinity. In case of a tie, you may decide which person you choose.

In addition, if the character with whom you have the highest Affinity is dead, you may not choose them (except Armin).

If your combined Affinity with Eren and Armin is 5 or more, go to 308.

If your Affinity with Mikasa is 4 or more, go to 301.

If your Affinity with Jean is 3 or more, go to 206.

If your Affinity with Krista is 3 or more, go to 310.

If your Affinity with Sasha is 3 or more, go to 309.

If none of the above applies, go to 315.

In addition, **if both Franz and Hannah are alive**, you may go to **200**. This ending may occur along with another ending.

•308

If Armin Arlert is…

Alive, go to 305

Dead, go to 215

After the battle. You and Sasha are walking through the streets of Trost.

The evacuated populace is crammed into temporary shelters on the far side of the inner wall. It will be some time before the town looks anything like it used to. There is a painful time of rebuilding to come.

But everyone is alive. All those people—you soldiers put your lives on the line and saved them.

"Hey, you two! Thank you!"

A little girl calls out to you and Sasha. You swell with pride.

But Sasha is looking at the girl with a greedy glint in her eyes. She seems to be looking at the bread ration in the girl's hand.

"Umm, you're welcome. To thank me, maybe you could give me some of that—"

You rush to drag Sasha away. Imagine, asking for food from a little evacuee girl.

"Aww. We're heroes, remember? We saved this town. And they're just gonna let us starve?"

You lead Sasha up on the wall as she complains. You take out the field ration you've been saving for just such an occasion.

"Oh, wow! Are you an angel? Or even a god?"

With that, she wolfs down your precious food. You'd hoped she might leave half for you, but in moments most of it is gone…

Sasha seems to feel a twinge of guilt when she's done eating, because she looks at you apologetically.

"Er. Um…"

She's wracking her brain for something to say. Eventually, this is what she comes up with:

"Oh, yeah! My home is a village in the woods, so I'm a pretty good hunter. There's not as much to hunt now on account of the Titans, but if we ever get a chance, I'll share some of the meat from my catch with you."

It seems to be her way of showing gratitude. But then, "some" also seems just like her. She plans to eat most of it herself…

But this is the first time you've heard her talk about this. You hope you can visit her village some day.

You look out over Trost District.

For a moment, it's peaceful.

You're sure one day you'll cherish simple conversations like this.

(The End / Sasha Blouse's Promise)

You survive the battle, but death was so near the entire time. Things look different now.

For example, the girl, Krista Lenz.

She's petite and pretty, with a kind heart. Those things make her popular, and in training she was sort of the unit's mascot.

Now…it's different. She's still lovely, and still acts the part of a compassionate girl, but you can't help thinking it's not the real her. In fact, you noticed how her impulse to kindness caused her to ignore danger on the battlefield.

"Hey, you. What are you staring at my Krista for?"

It's the freckled girl. She gives you a poke and a glare.

During training, you wondered why such an ill-tempered girl would have been so close to someone like Krista… But maybe she caught on to who Krista was long before you did.

If you could learn more about who the girl really is, maybe you could be better friends with her, too.

"Hmm." The freckled girl stares openly at you. Then, as if by intuition, she says, "Whatever happens after this, trust her."

This girl might just be better than she looks, too.

Hrm. What was her name again?

"It's Ymir. You could at least remember a person's name," she says, but then shrugs.

You would eventually find out who she truly was. But not for a very long time.

(The End / The Girl Who Hid Her True Self)

● **311**

A short while later, you find yourself in a dilemma.

So many things have happened since then. You've joined the Survey Corps. You've even become a member of the so-called "Squad Levi," serving directly under the famous captain—along with several of your other friends and fellow survivors.

If that were all, you would be quite proud of yourself.

But instead, you are being hounded by the First Interior Squad of the

Military Police Brigade. They are chasing you down with vertical maneuvering equipment designed for use against humans, bent on wiping all of you out. The papers are publishing nonsense claiming the Survey Corps rebelled against the king and killed innocent people.

You were all caught in a trap. You are bereft of friends among both the military and the populace.

How did this happen? With no way of resupplying and scant information, you are unable to mount an effective response. If only you had an ally—so much as a merchant who would cooperate with you... Where did you go wrong?

But to your worries, Captain Levi says quietly:

"Even I don't know when I've made the right choice and when the wrong in my life so far. The most any of us can do is try to act in a way that leaves us without regrets."

You nod. The First Interior Squad forces encircling you begin to move. You prepare to fight this hopeless battle with your comrades at your side...

(Bitter End / The Death of a Merchant)

●312

You lie on the ground, covered in blood. You can't feel your legs— they were bitten off by a Titan.

You're going to die.

At least this is better than being devoured or swallowed alive by a

Titan...you think.

How did the battle turn out, anyway?

The next thing you know, you're in someone's arms. Short in stature, with piercing eyes—it's Captain Levi.

His hands and uniform are drenched with your blood. But he doesn't flinch, doesn't even seem to mind, despite the fact that he's supposed to be a bit of a clean freak. "The plan worked," he tells you, with as much brevity and dispassion as ever. "You did your duty with honor."

Most people probably have no idea that he would take the time to hold a nameless soldier, talk to them. He must have cared for many dying boys and girls in his time.

"You've done more than enough...and you'll do more. The resolve you leave behind will give me strength. I swear to you... I will eradicate the Titans!!"

As you breathe your last, you smile.

Does the Captain see it?

(The End / No Regrets)

● **313**

Jean Kirstein learned a great deal from the battle. But in the end, he applied to the Military Police Brigade. Complete with the same bad attitude he had in training.

You went into the Military Police, too. In principle, only the top ten graduates of any class are eligible to join the MPs, but because many of the top scorers in your class didn't apply to the unit, you were allowed in based on your actions in the Battle of Trost.

You are assigned to the Military Police unit in Stohess District of Wall Sheena—in the interior.

This is where you see firsthand the corruption of the Military Police Brigade. They are supposed to be the elite of the elite, protecting the interior and the royal capital, but you see them drinking before noon, foisting not only random chores but their actual duties on you new recruits.

Jean mixed quite well with this way of life outwardly, but inside he was stewing.

His anger was directed not at the disgraceful conduct of his superior officers or the organization as a whole, but at your fellow recruit, Marlowe.

Marlowe Freudenberg is a serious boy with a strong sense of right and wrong, convinced that he is going to reform the Military Police. Jean does not find this amusing, and finally confronts him.

"You, straighten out the MPs? Dammit, there are idiots like you even here?!"

Right now he's got Marlowe by the collar again. Marlowe, being Marlowe, won't back down a step.

"Ha ha ha! Glad to see you two getting along!"

Another new recruit, a girl named Hitch, is laughing uproariously.

(Another End / Jean of the Military Police)

252 •313

You wonder how much time passed in the fighting.

You dart about, swinging your blade for all you're worth. What's become of the other soldiers, of your friends, you have no idea.

There's a rumble from far off. That's the direction of the gate.

As you maneuver through the sky, the air you fly through is the same air that brings you word.

You catch a glimpse of the sky, where your eye is drawn to a yellow line.

A signal flare. Yellow smoke—the sign that a plan has succeeded.

"They did it!" someone shouts.

People have climbed up on the nearby rooftops. They cheer, or shout that you should go help Eren; others head for the gate themselves.

The plan worked.

The city is still overrun with Titans. At this moment, soldiers are still being overpowered by the monsters, killed and eaten. The tragedy of this battle is still playing out.

But you are triumphant.

(**Mark Ian Dietrich and Mitabi Jarnach dead**. Go to **288**.)

You decide to join the Garrison. Among other things, this battle taught you how important it is to protect the people inside the walls. That experience also gets you assigned to the Trost District unit.

And so...

Today, you're once more assigned to the top of the city's wall.

"Hey, rookie. How ya doin'?" One of the more experienced soldiers, Mr. Hannes, calls out to you. "Well, don't go crazy. Relax a little."

Then he laughs. He's an easygoing guy.

"I'll thank you not to encourage laziness in my troops."

That's your commanding officer, Squad Leader Rico. She glares at him.

Mr. Hannes smiles indulgently. She gives him a thin smile in return. You were all in different places, but all of you came through that battle and saved this town.

Mr. Hannes looks down at the gate, still blocked by the boulder, and murmurs fondly, "I wonder if Eren's doing all right."

(The End / Joining the Garrison)

A Kodansha Comics Trade Paperback Original
Attack on Titan Choose Your Path Adventure—Year 850: Last Stand at Wall Rose copyright © 2015 Tomoyuki Fujinami
English translation copyright © 2017 Tomoyuki Fujinami

All rights reserved.

Published in the United States by Kodansha Comics, an imprint of Kodansha USA Publishing, LLC, New York.

Publication rights for this English edition arranged through Kodansha Ltd, Tokyo.

First published in Japan in 2015 by Kodansha Ltd., Tokyo as *Shingeki no kyojin geemu bukku: Wooru Rooze Shishu Meirei 850.*

ISBN 978-1-63236-415-9

Original cover design by Takashi Shimoyama (Red Rooster)

Printed in the United States of America.

www.kodanshacomics.com

9 8 7 6 5 4 3 2 1
Translation: Kevin Steinbach
Layout: AndWorld Design
Editorial Assistance: Tiff Ferentini
Editing: Paul Starr
Kodansha Comics edition cover design by Phil Balsman